The Vanishing Glaciers of Patagonia

100 years in retrospect

Explorers, their stories, their photographs and climate change

Based on
'An Adventure Sail to Patagonia' by H N Pallin
translated by Unn Hellsten, Åsa Hellsten and Ulf Hellsten

With extracts from
'The Letters of Allan Bäckman to his Wife Elna'
provided by John Hedenström

With additional material from
Commander Pringle Stokes RN (of HMS *Beagle*), Dr Hans Steffen,
Professor Otto Nordenskjöld, Crispin Agnew
and Professor Stephan Harrison

Compiled, edited and with additional information by
Martin Sessions

Publishers:
Inspiring Publishers
P.O. Box 159 Calwell ACT 2905, Australia.
Email: inspiringpublishers@gmail.com

National Library of Australia Cataloguing-in-Publication entry

Author: **Martin Sessions**

Title: **The Vanishing Glaciers of Patagonia:** 100 years in retrospect

ISBN: 978-1-922792-31-0 (Print)

ISBN: 978-1-922792-32-7 (Hardcover)

ISBN: 978-1-922792-33-4 (eBook)

✦
Synopsis

In 1839, Charles Darwin remarked, with some amazement, about the occurrence of glaciers at sea level in the Gulf of Penas, latitude 46° 40'. One glacier he referred to was the San Quintin Glacier. This remark must have triggered the interest of Professor Otto Nordenskjöld, the famed Swedish explorer and geographer. In 1920, Professor Nordenskjöld led a small expedition to explore and document remote parts of South America. The second phase was to the ice covered terrain of Chilean Patagonia, specifically the North Patagonian Icefield and its largest glacier, the San Quintin.

This is the story of that episode as told by Nils Pallin, the expedition's surveyor, with additional extracts illustrating the challenges they faced in this unforgiving region from Allan Bäckman's letters. In the process of researching this expedition, 200 uncaptioned photographs were assembled and a selection has been added to enhance this story. A chronology of significant events affecting the region has been included together with a summary of subsequent exploration.

Whilst Professor Nordenskjöld may have left this dynamic region feeling that the expedition had not achieved as much as it might have done due to the challenges of the terrain and the inhospitable weather, the expedition's photographs were later used to reveal the mind shatteringly fast disappearance of the

3

smaller glaciers together with the rapid thinning of the largest glacier, the San Quintin.

Left to right: Nils Pallin, Allan Bäckman,
Professor Otto Nordenskjöld and Sten von Rosen

✧

In memory of the expeditioners

Professor Otto Nordenskjöld

H N Pallin

Allan Bäckman

Sten von Rosen

Livorio, Pedro and Olegari

✧ Contents

✧
Preface

This book is primarily about the impressive Glacier San Quintin, the largest glacier of the North Patagonian Icefield in a pretty inaccessible part of the West Coast of Chilean Patagonia. Glacier San Quintin was accessed for the

*Map of South America showing
location of Kelly Inlet*

first time in 1920/21 from Kelly Inlet by a Swedish expedition led by Professor Otto Nordenskjold. Whilst Kelly Inlet is only about 60 km from the frequently visited Laguna San Rafael with its glacier that calves at sea level, getting to Kelly Inlet is significantly harder.

My involvement with Glacier San Quintin and Kelly Inlet started in 1971 when I applied for a position on the (British) Joint Services Expedition to Chilean Patagonia to take place in the southern summer of 1972/73, led by Crispin Agnew. My role was to investigate some of the physical features of a glacier and to run the meteorological program. As a result, I researched some of the original articles on the area including H N (Nils) Pallin's 'Mountains And Glaciers In West Patagonia', published in *Alpine Journal* No. 45 (1933) and Dr Hans Steffen's *Patagonia Occidental* (1909).

In 1999, following an e-mail from Charles Warren of the University of St Andrews, I decided that a return trip to Kelly Inlet was warranted to see how Glacier Benito, the glacier studied in 1972/73, was changing. After visits to Neil Glasser (University of Wales Aberystwyth) and Stephan Harrison (at Coventry University at that time) together with a reconnaissance to Coyhaique in Chile in 2006, I was able to formulate plans for and execute a month long expedition to Kelly Inlet in 2007. In particular, I was able to recruit two excellent husband-and-wife teams. Olaf Wündrich and Jammie Valdivia played major roles in the venture. Graham Hornsey and Carmen Gloria Monjes provided all the necessary logistics and logistic support including finding the transport at the last moment. Vanessa Winchester from Oxford University participated in the expedition and authored the subsequent paper on the results. Although we were not able to walk to the former 'end of summer season' snow line, we established physically that the glacier was thinning extremely rapidly in its lower region. A repeat trip was made in 2011 which re-enforced our earlier measurements.

In March 2016, an accomplished Chilean mountaineer, Camilo Rada, contacted me concerning the routes taken by the 1972/73 expedition on the North Patagonian Icefield and the names of certain peaks. In the process he alerted me to the fact that three albums of Nils Pallin's photographs from 1920/21 were up for sale on Vancouver Island, Canada, near where he was studying for his PhD at the time. By the time we interrogated the seller, the albums had been sold. A few months later we discovered that they had been purchased by the University of California Library, Special Collections at Santa Barbara.

One important task was still outstanding on Glacier Benito which was to use GPS technology to remeasure a 6.5 kilometre profile across the glacier at about the 1972/73 'end of summer season' snow line, which I called the 'Levels'. In 2017, I decided to hire a helicopter to fly us up to the site on Glacier Benito. As we had the opportunity to fly near the summit where Nils Pallin took some photographs, I negotiated with University of California Library, Special Collections to obtain digital scans of the third album which contained photographs of the relevant glaciers. The next requirement was to obtain the 'copyright' permission to use the photographs which rests with the descendants of Nils Pallin. Using the services of *Find Your Swedish Ancestry* (Johan Grönberg), I was provided with the contact details of three of Nils Pallin's grandchildren, Ulf, Unn and Åsa. We commenced corresponding with each other and they provided me with an English translation of the articles that Nils Pallin wrote on return to Sweden which forms the core of this book.

At the end of the successful, helicopter-supported trip to Glacier Benito in 2017 to measure the 'Levels', I mentioned to Gabriela Gómez González, the Corporación Nacional Forestal's (CONAF) person in charge of the protected wildlands of the Aysén Province, that the 100th anniversary of Professor Otto Nordenskjöld's 1920/21 Swedish expedition was approaching. I resolved to assemble more material about the expedition, not least for it to be lodged with the CONAF's offices, tourist sites and the Coyhaique Library for use by officials, rangers, researchers and tourists.

One of the many interesting features that make up this part of the world had been bothering me; this concerned the 'little ice age'. Moraines associated with the 'little ice age' on both Glacier San Quintin and Glacier Benito were dated to about 1850. The question was over what period were the glaciers advancing to create this moraine formation? In particular, I was interested in what early British hydrographers had seen. Whilst surfing the web, I came across an article about Commander Pringle Stokes's last journal (1828) which ended up in the Mitchell Library of New South Wales, in Sydney, Australia. An emotional visit was made to view the journal and photograph pages relevant to Kelly Inlet. The next step was to view the charts of the West Coast of Patagonia, produced by Stokes and others. I went to the UK Hydrographic Office, Taunton. The last chart to be shown to me on my visit was the original 1830 chart which clearly depicts Glacier San Rafael and Glacier San Quintin.

As I was assembling this story of the 1920/21 expedition, I wanted more information about two participants, Allan Bäckman and Sten von Rosen. I employed the services of *Find Your Swedish Ancestry* again. Besides providing me with the obituaries, Johan Grönberg found an item relevant to the descendants of Otto Nordenskjölds's 'club' and a remark that

Allan Bäckman's grandson, John Hedenström, was writing a book about his grandfather's participation in the 1920/21 Swedish expedition to South America using letters that Allan had sent his wife. We started corresponding and swapping material and information, and as a result, I am able to add some passages from these letters to enhance Nils Pallin's tale, together with more photographs. Note that the tense changes in these letters in diary form depending on whether he was describing events, his thoughts or future activities.

In one of Allan Bäckman's letters, he talks about the value of his meteorological observations made during the expedition and suggests that this was the main result to come out of the expedition. In fact, the photographs of the glaciers and scenery are more important with the advent of the rapid warming in the region and the consequent loss of ice. For this reason, many photographs are included to illustrate what was seen even though they may be of low quality.

The Professor, Nils Pallin and Allan Bäckman walked on Glacier San Quintin at a place where no one has walked on the glacier since and is unlikely to do so for maybe many years, if ever. They crossed the mountain range using a route that is unlikely to be used again. They saw scenery that won't look like what they saw for maybe many hundreds or even thousands of years. For these reasons, the preservation of this record is important.

I am responsible for the opinions and observations presented in the Prologue, Epilogue and Notes as well as the interpretation of parts of the translation of Nils Pallin's story and Allan Bäckman's letters.

Martin Sessions
December 2021

✧
Prologue

O ur story starts with a terrible tragedy, a shipwreck. Only a few members of a crew of over 248 who sailed from England and 150 who reached shore from the wrecked ship returned to their homes; the rest perished mainly from starvation or scurvy in a hostile land. HMS *Wager* was one of eight ships that formed Commodore Anson's squadron that left England on 18th September 1740 with the purpose of capturing Spanish ports on the west coast of South America and also undertaking some trade in friendly ports. By April 1741[01], the squadron had rounded Cape Horn and were travelling up the west coast of South America. A severe storm scattered the ships on 24th April. At 4 am on 14th May 1741, the *Wager* struck rocks off an island that was later to be named Wager Island in the Guayaneco Archipelago. About 150 men reached shore.

Then followed a period of mayhem, drunkenness, mutiny, treachery, starvation often leading to death, ingenuity and assistance from the indigenous peoples[02]. One of the crew who returned to his home was John Byron aged 18 when the *Wager* grounded, and who subsequently became a vice admiral. In 1768, he published his narrative of the events *Narrative of the Hon. John Byron; Being an Account of the Shipwreck of The Wager; and the Subsequent Adventures of Her Crew* which was republished in 1830 in a more readable format[03]. The significance of this narrative increased because Byron's grandson

15

was Lord George Byron, the famous poet. However, his narrative did contain many very similar passages to the narrative written earlier by Alexander Campbell (17 years old at the time of the grounding) titled *Adventures of Capt. Cheap, the Hon. Mr. Byron, Lieut. Hamilton, Alexander Campbell and others, late of his Majesty's ship the Wager* published in 1747[04].

Byron's frontpiece, 'Loss of Wager, 1768, 2nd Edition 1769

Byron, Campbell and their captain (Captain Cheap) and 17 others travelled north from Wager Island, leaving on 15th December 1741. Their aim was to go round Cabo Raper to the north-west of Golfo de Penas. After six weeks of trying to get around the stormy cape and failing, starving in the process, they returned to where they had started from. On 6th March

1742, a Spanish speaking native of Chiloe (Chonos) led them across Golfo de Penas to Golfo de San Tadeo. Some days later, the four survivors travelled up the San Tadeo River, crossed the Istmo de Ofqui, followed by crossing Laguna San Rafael, then travelled north in the Rio Tempanos and into the Gulfo de Elefantes on their way to Chiloe (Map of Golfo de Penas – Route 1). Whilst it appears that neither Byron nor Campbell visited Kelly Inlet, they did describe how the Chonos canoes (or dalcas) were dissembled to cross land. The canoes were made of three or five planks sewed together with 'supple-jack'.

Byron and Campbell travelled in bigger and more seaworthy boats than the indigenous people around Golfo de Penas namely a barge and a yawl. Byron described the conditions as 'torrents of rain', 'vast sea and surf' and 'very high sea breaking with great fury upon this coast'. He once saw a canoe at sea and remarked 'on how unusual it was for Indians to venture out in so mountainous sea'. Finally, he noted that the peoples were 'frequently obliged to carry them (canoes) overland, through thick woods, to avoid doubling capes and headlands in sea where no open boat could live'. The dangerous conditions were highlighted to Campbell when 'the wind shifted in an instant, a great sea (wave) tumbled into the bay, began to break and sank the yawl'.

The significance of Byron's and Campbell's stories was that interest in the formidable West Patagonia region grew substantially in the English speaking world and was to influence subsequent explorations of this remote and tempestuous region.

Padre Agueros[05], Dr Hans Steffen[06], Captain Herman Ferrer Fouga[07] and others list several 'expeditions' that crossed the Istmo de Ofqui en route to Guayaneco Archipelago, the Wellington Archipelago and Messier Canal region as summarised below (Map of Golfo de Penas – Route 2).

TABLE: 'Expeditions' that crossed the Istmo de Ofqui

YEAR	EXPEDITION DETAILS
1674	Bartolomé Diez Gallardo travelled to Laguna San Rafael, Istmo de Ofqui and Lucac River. Advanced to Ayautau Islands in the south of Golfo de Penas and saw the Guayaneco Archipelago.
1675	Antonio de Vea crossed Istmo de Ofqui and observed glaciers that advanced to Laguna San Rafael. Possible visit to San Xavier Island and northern end of Wellington Archipelago.
1742	Grounding and loss of HMS *Wager* in the Guayaneco Archipelago. Byron, Campbell and others from the crew travelled north from the Guayanecos Islands, eventually arriving at Chiloe.
1744	Mateo Abraham Edward with Father Pedro Flores and 160 men in 11 canoes salvaged 14 cannons and other items from the *Wager* during a four-month expedition starting from Chiloe[08].
1750	Mateo Abraham Edward produced a chart of the islands between Chiloe and the Straits of Magellan.
1766	Fr Jose Garcia Alsue embarked on a six-month trip after envoys had arrived with Calens (Messier Canal region). Headed south in five canoes, 34 indigenous peoples and five Spaniards via Istmo de Ofqui to eastern and southern edges of Gulfo de Penas including Guayaneco Archipelago and northern part of Fallos Canal and Estero Messier 'end unknown'[09].

1768	Jose de Sotomayor with pilot Francisco Hipolito Machado went to Istmo de Ofqui with 60 men for two weeks. Went on to Guayaneco Archipelago, northern end of Messier Canal, Puerto Santa Barbara on Isla Campana (49th parallel). Returned via Istmo de Ofqui. Chart reproduced by Jose de Moraleda.
1768	Lieutenant Pedro Mancilla and pilot Cosme Ugarte reportedly went south to 53° 19'.
1778	Fr Benito Marin and Br Julian Real with three canoes via Istmo de Ofqui discovered bays and fjords of mainland at 47th parallel then travelled to Guayaneco Archipelago, Messier Canal and Boca de Canales. Inlets Benito and Julian in Estero Jesuitas were named after them.
1780	Fr Francisco Menedez and Fr Ignacio Vargas travelled along shores of Gulfo de Penas to Ayautau Islands and Guayaneco Archipelago.

Of the above expeditions, only three explorers made specific reference to a glacier in Laguna San Rafael. The first was Antoia de Vea in 1675 and the second was Fr Jose Garcia Alsue. Reference to ice in the Laguna San Rafael is also made by Agueros[05] in the chapter describing Fr Benito Marin's and Br Julian Real's expedition. It refers to the 'many snow cliffs that were found, some large, some small, and others medium'. Machodo and later Jose de Moraleda[07], who was in the area between 1787 and 1796, produced surveys, charts and a description of the region. But little evidence of the extensive, west-flowing glaciers of the North Patagonian Icefield was included.

Of relevance to our story is how Glacier Benito, which Pallin called South Glacier, came to be named. On 22nd and 23rd December 1778[05], Fr Benito Marin and Br Julian Real with their expedition were located near Xavier Island at a place called San Salvador on the 'Costa de la Tierra-Firme' (the 'Main Land'). Between the 23rd and 30th Don Pedro, one of the expedition pilots explored what was to be named Fiordo Jesuitas and the Benito and Julian Inlets (Map of Golfo de Penas – Route 3).

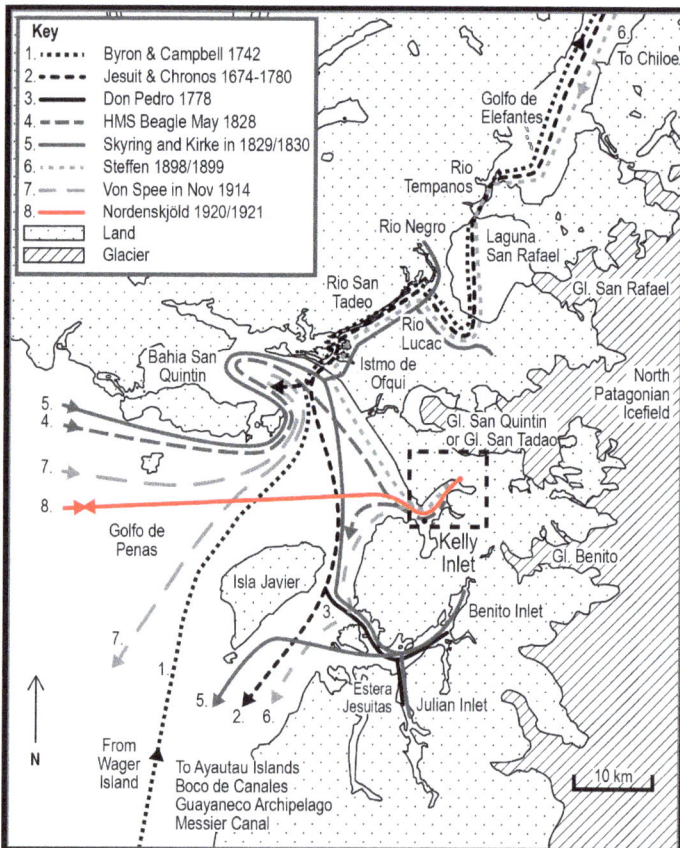

Map of Golfo de Penas showing the routes taken by many of the early explorers[10]

After all the activities up to 1780, the story of events in Golfo de Penas goes quiet until 1828. What happened? Firstly, the Jesuit priests on Chiloe were replaced by Franciscans who were less committed to recruiting more indigenous peoples to Christianity[06]. Next, the Royal Governor of Chiloe, Antonio Narciso de Santa María (1749 to 1761), introduced a policy to depopulate the Guaitecas Archipelago so that Chiloe could be better defended. Then the Chilean war of independence started in 1812 and Chiloe was effectively one of very few Spanish outposts on the Chilean coast until it joined the new Republic of Chile in 1826. With chaos occurring in Europe due to Bonaparte's campaigns in Spain, few Spanish maritime resources could be allocated to looking after far away Chiloe. Also, the land route from Santiago to Puerto Montt and on to Chiloe was cut for many years by the Mapuches[11].

In terms of indigenous peoples travelling south from Chiloe via the Istmo de Ofqui, a more significant event occurred which interfered with their travel route. Alberto Areneda[12] and others reviewed the documented historical evidence for changes in extent of Glacier San Rafael and deduced that up to 1766, the glacier was 'in its valley'. The next documented visit after that was by Simpson in 1871 where the glacier was found to have extended about 8 km across Laguna San Rafael. The fact that the glacier would have been in its valley in the early 1700s is also supported by the narratives of Byron and Campbell and many others who made no mention of seeing a glacier or even 'bergy bits'.

Questions arise from the change in position of the ice front of Glacier San Rafael between 1766 and 1871. Was the expansion over a short period or a long period? If over a short period, when did the expansion start? When did it reach its zenith?

A clue may be found from the coring of the Great Barrier Reef off Queensland, Australia, by the University of Edinburgh[13]. In the decades between 1700 and 1810 there were on average three coral bleaching events in each decade. The decade 1820 had no bleaching events and the decades 1830 to 1860 each had one bleaching event. A major 'geographical' event occurred at the beginning of the 1800s causing the region, indeed the world, to cool.

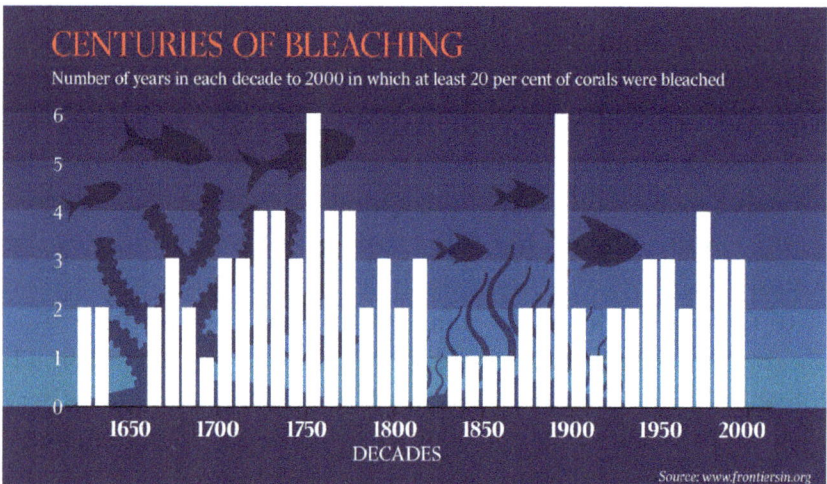

History of Coral Bleaching, Glasgow Edinburgh Frontiers, Marine Science[13]

On 10th April 1815, the modern world experienced its most powerful, natural explosion. Mount Tambora (8° 15' 0" S, 118° 0' 0" E), on the island of Sumbawa in present day Indonesia exploded with a devastating effect[14]. The eruption column is estimated to have reached the stratosphere at an altitude of more than 43 kilometres. The coarser ash particles settled out one to two weeks after the eruptions, but the finer ash particles stayed in the atmosphere from a few months to a few years at altitudes of 10 to 30 kilometres. During

the northern hemisphere summer of 1816, global temperatures cooled by 0.53°C. The 1815 eruption occurred during a
'Dalton Minimum', a period of unusually low solar radiation.
The effect in the Northern Hemisphere was dramatic with
severe famine affecting many people. In particular, in western Switzerland, the summers of 1816 and 1817 were so cold
that an ice dam formed below a tongue of the Giétro Glacier
high in the Val de Bagnes. Despite engineer Ignaz Venetz's
efforts to drain the growing lake, the ice dam collapsed cat-
astrophically in June 1818, killing 40 people. Another effect
along the seaboards of continents was significantly increased
precipitation.

Mount Tambora is in the Southern Hemisphere. With
the general atmospheric circulation from west to east and
Patagonia being closer to Mount Tambora than Europe, south
of the Equator in South America may have experienced a
greater climatic change than that experienced in Europe.

Another major volcanic explosion in the South Pacific region
was identified from Greenland ice cores dating to 1808/1809
which may have started the cooling effect in the North
Patagonian Icefield a few years earlier. The volcano responsible for this event has not been identified, but its atmospheric
effects were observed in Bogota and Lima[15].

Were these two major volcanic eruptions responsible
for a major advance of outflowing glaciers from the North
Patagonian Icefield?

The first documented visit to Kelly Inlet was by the British
survey ship, HMS *Beagle*, under the command of Commander
Pringle Stokes RN on 25th May 1828, with Lieutenant W G
Skyring as the assistant surveyor (Map of Golfo de Penas –
Route 4). One of the reasons for the survey work along this
coast was to find out what had happened to the *Wager*. Stokes's

original journal[16] is in the New South Wales State Library. The
best description is from his journal[17].

HMS *Beagle,* 23rd May 1828

On an amendment (change) of the weather about 9 AM, we
weighed anchor (in San Quintin's Sound) and made sail WSW
magnetic along the northern shores of San Quintin's Sound . . . .
Its shores are thickly wooded, with shapely and well grown trees;
the land near the shores for the most part is low, rising into
mountainous peaks a little distance in the interior, of which some
are from 12 to 15 hundred (feet) high, but not craggy. Various
streams of water were observed descending from the mountains
and reaching to the shores. A ship, as soon as she gets a couple
of miles to the NW of a smallish island, marked in the chart, Dead
Tree Island, (from the many bare trunks and branches standing
on it) will be perfectly landlocked, and sheltered from the sea; in
all parts of it, is anchorage depth on a muddy or sandy bottom:
so that if Saint Quintin's Sound or Inlet were situated in quarter
of the world where the advantages it offers to shipping might
be profited by, it would be deemed a fine spacious and secured
Harbour.

Whales were numerous at the mouth of the Inlet, and some
hair seals were seen. Having traced this sound to its termination
we bore up, and, passing this time to the westward of Dead Tree
Island, sailed ESE magnetic for an inlet in the North Eastern Shore
of the Gulf bearing from the North end of and distant from San
Xavier Island two leagues, for the purpose of examining it for an
anchorage.

In this inlet we affected an anchorage in the course of the afternoon; I have given a detailed description of it in the following page,
and shall now only add that though it affords anchoring depth, it
is by no means to be recommended as a Harbour, for could there

be anything to lead a ship so far into the Gulf, the Sound of Saint Quintin would afford a much more eligible situation, as being easier to access and much more safe and sheltered.

Occurrences in Kelly's Harbour - 24th May 1828

Another four and twenty hours of incessant heavy rain and thick foggy weather. Between one and three in the morning, we had some smart showers of hail, sleet and snow which we found at daylight had well powdered the mountain tops around us; their fall was attended with a very sensible decrease of temperature. The thermometer varied from 35° to 45° (1.7°C to 7.2°C) during the day. Sheltered by the lofty mountains around the Harbour, we had the wind light at West, and WNW. It seemed we are anchored in the current of some considerable fresh water streams, for at half tide, the water alongside is perfectly fresh; it is of milky colour, and full of earthy particles.

Occurrences 25th May 1828

AM. A little after midnight a sudden change from heavy rain and thick fog to fine clear frosty weather. The thermometer fell to 30° (-1.1°C) and at daylight we found that a pellicle (thin film) of ice about the thickness of a dollar had formed in patches in all parts of the anchorage; we were becalmed by the high land of the Harbour, but from the direction of the clouds, the wind was in the north eastern quarter.

Immediately after daylight, two boats were employed in sounding and sketching the anchorage. They completed that service and returned on board by about 10 AM; upon which I weighed and made sail out of the Harbour. The wind was so light that it was past noon before we had cleared the entrance. I landed on its North point, with sextant and artificial horizon, and by the sun's meridian altitude determined its latitude as 46° 59' 08 South.

In the next page, I have given a full account and a sketched plan of this Harbour which I have called Kelly's Harbour[18], after a friend and brother officer, Captain B M Kelly, RN[19]. To Captain Kelly, I am indebted for my introduction to the leader of the expedition, Captain P P King, RN, FRS.

On clearing Kelly's Harbour, we steered SWbW magnetic until nearly abreast of the East end of San Xavier Island and then South magnetic in the channel between that island and the mainland . . .

In the North Eastern part of the Gulf of Penas West Coast of Patagonia - Kelly's Harbour

Kelly's Harbour (of which a sketch is annexed) and the North point of its entrance lies in latitude 46° 59′ 08″ South, and longitude . . . West. The land about the Harbour is high, rugged rocky and mountainous, but by no means devoid of verdure (lush, green vegetation); in the interior are lofty, peaked, and craggy ranges of snow covered mountains. The points of the entrance are low as compared with the adjacent land, and are thickly wooded. They lie of each other, N48E and S48W magnetic, distant 2 miles asunder, with a channel between them of from 40 to 35 fathoms depth of water, on a mud bottom and quite free from dangers and hold to a cable length of the rocky islets which lie at the distance of somewhat less than a quarter of a mile offshore on either hand. On approaching the fairway of the Harbour, the extraordinary muddy appearance of the water is rather startling; the discoloration, however, proceeds only from the freshes of the rivers and streams within; so far from any shallowness, 30 fathoms will be found the least depth until at a distance of two or three cable lengths of the anchorage indicated by the anchors in the sketch. ESE magnetic is the course in, until between the North point, and a narrow sound, or inlet, on the starboard hand having five or six thickly wooded islets at its mouth; then haul up along the larboard (port) or North Western shore of the Harbour, as close as you please, and when the North point is well locked on, the South point of the entrance bearing S48W magnetic, anchor as soon as a depth of water is convenient.

The *Beagle* was anchored in 22 fathoms, within a cable and a half of a sandy spit which runs off the western end of a highish thickly wooded island at the North end of the Harbour; the points of the entrance looked as above mentioned. The holding ground is an uncommonly tenacious mud; we found great difficulty in heaving up our anchor, although we had the advantage of Captain Charles Phillips's admirable 'Patent Capstan'. Wood for fuel, and good freshwater, this Harbour affords in abundance; but with the exception of shelter, it affords nothing more. Environment with lofty mountains (some of them from 14 to 15 hundred feet high), and ice filled valleys and ravines, it is chilly, damp, and dreary. A very few birds, of the aquatic kinds common in these parts, and a small number of hair sales, comprised all we saw of animated nature; not a trace of human beings.

For knowing Kelly's Harbour, there is a glacier, which if it be, as from its compact and majestic appearances, I think it is, perpetual, affords a capital leading mark. This glacier[20] is a large field of ice lying on the low point of the coast about a couple of miles to the northward of the Harbour, and is sufficiently remarkable as there is no permanent ice or snow on the low part of the coast to the south of the Harbour, even at the time of our visit, a period distance less than a month from the winter.

The water at our Anchorage was perfectly fresh alongside at 1/2 tide; but it was too full of earthly particles to be fit for immediate use; recourse for a supply must be had to the stream marked 'C' in the sketch.

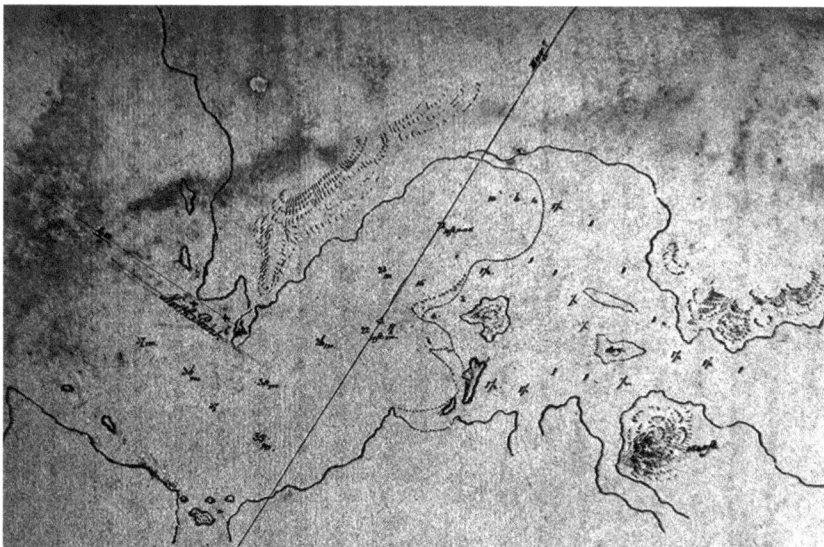

The first sketch of Kelly Harbour from Stokes's journal[16]

Stokes found surveying the coast in mid-winter very challenging and was very unhappy that he could not accomplish what he was required to achieve. As a result, he tragically took his life in August 1828. That tragedy triggered an interesting sequence of events. Captain P P King, in command of the surveying expedition, wanted to promote Lieutenant Skyring to command HMS *Beagle*. He was overruled by Rear Admiral Sir Robert Waller Otway who appointed a very capable Lieutenant, Robert Fitz-Roy, on his staff instead[21]. Fitz-Roy wanted a person with a similar mind to accompany him on his voyages so selected Charles Darwin and the rest is history.

HMS *Adventure* returned to this coastline in summertime at the end of 1829 and this time Lieutenant Skyring did some more detailed surveys in the sloop *Adelaide*[17]. In particular he and Mr Kirke explored the San Tadeo River in an attempt to find out where Byron, Campbell and others crossed from the river to Laguna San Rafael (Map of Golfo de Penas – Route 5). During their four day trip up river in a whale boat, they discovered the 'Black River' (Rio Negro), then went up Rio Lucac until they came within two miles (3 km) of the foot of a mountain. As a result of this trip, they were able to sketch two large glaciers (flowing from 'Lofty Glacier') that Darwin used to espouse the fact that these glaciers were the closest to the equator that reached sea level[22]. Mr Kirke also explored the Estero Jesuitas together with Benito Inlet and Julian Inlet[23]. When exploring Estero Jesuitas, Mr. Kirke said, 'There are two openings opposite Xavier Island, on the main land; the northernmost runs through high land, and is terminated by a low sandy beach, with a river in the middle, running from a large glacier[24]; the southern inlet is ended by high mountainous land.' Of particular note is the fact that they did not find any indigenous people in the northern part of Golfo de Penas whilst Byron and Campbell had noted many contacts with these people when they were there.

An original chart exists at the UK Hydrographic Office dated 1830 showing the results of Stokes, Skyring and Kirke's hydrographic surveys[25]. The chart would have been used by Darwin when he wrote Volume 3 of the *Narrative (Journal and Remarks, 1832—1836)*[22] and in particular the extract from the chart at page 285. This chart is the first known sketch of the North Patagonian Icefield as we know it today and it helps substantiate that Glacier San Rafael had advanced considerably by 1829.

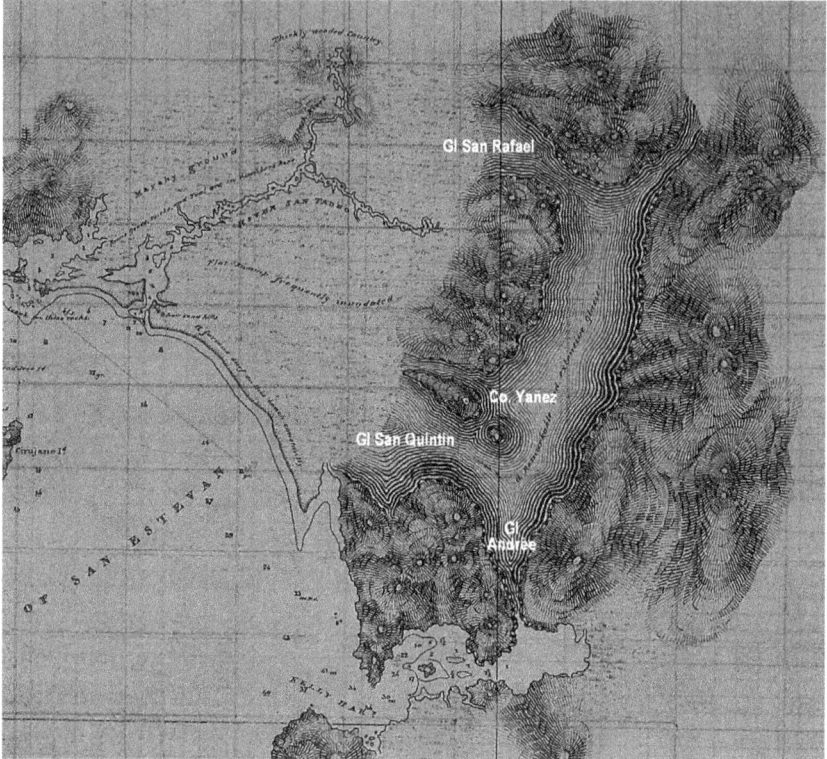

Extract of chart created by Stokes, Skyring and Kirke dated 1830

The northern glacier flowing to low land is Glacier San Rafael and the southern one is Glacier San Quintin

Glacier San Quintin's maximum advance in the 'modern' era was subsequently dated as 1850, by Winchester and Harrison[26] using tree ring analysis.

The next documented visit to Kelly Inlet before the 1920/21 Swedish expedition was by Dr Hans Steffen in 1898 as part of his work for the Border Commission[27]. Steffen was Professor of the Pedagogical Institute, Member of the University of Chile, and described his role as former technical advisor to the Chilean

Delegation before the Arbitration Court of Limits in London. He undertook sea-based exploration with the aim of finding a route through the mountain range to the Eastern pampas. They went south via Laguna San Rafael and Rio San Tadeo to the Gulfo de Penas, then called in to Kelly Inlet (Map of Golfo de Penas – Route 6). The map below details Dr Steffen's route of investigation from his original book, *Patagonia Occidental* published in 1910.

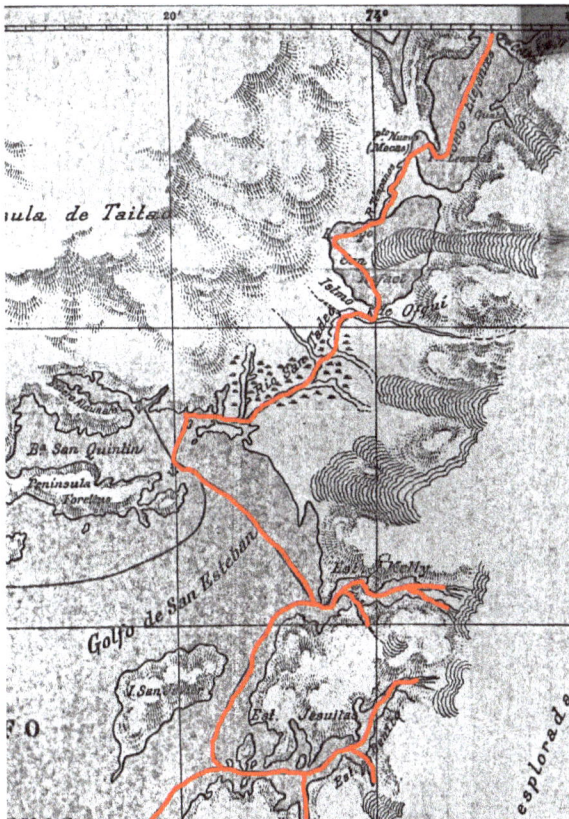

Dr Steffen's route in 1898 to investigate routes to the interior through the Cordillera[27]

Of interest is the fact that a third 'significant' glacier is shown between Glacier San Rafael, flowing into Laguna San Rafael and Glacier San Quintin just north of Estero Kelly[28]. In fact, this 'glacier' is due to a mismatch between the latitudes measured by Skyring in 1829 and Enrique Simpson who surveyed Laguna San Rafael in 1871 when Glacier San Rafael had spread eight kilometres across the tidal lake.

For the crossing of the Istmo de Ofqui, Steffen and his team used a track created by José Pinto de Compu, with the assistance of several Chilotes a couple of years earlier when searching for gold in the southern shores of the Taitao Peninsula. Steffen thought that the track used by the Chonos and Spanish explorers lay a small distance to the west of their route but no evidence of such a track could be found. After navigating down the Lucac and San Tadeo Rivers in small boats, Steffen and his team re-joined the support ship, the *Pisagua*, which had sailed around Cabo Raper and then moved on to Kelly Inlet.

A translated extract from Steffen's *Occidental Patagonia* 1909 edition of his visit to Kelly Inlet follows[27].

At 6 A.M. on the 12th December we set sail from San Quintin with a low barometer and a strong north wind, to make the crossing to the Kelly Estuary[28], which forms the closest entrance to the sea on the continental coast of the Gulf of Penas[29], and which, according to the description of Fitzroy, is one of the most desolate and inhospitable places of the entire coast.

We passed between the Forelius peninsula [20] and a rocky island in front, leaving a very long lowland *vega*[30] to the left, at the southwestern end of which ends a branch of the same large glacier we had observed during navigation on the San Tadeo River. On its surface and lower edge can be seen what we missed at the other ice rivers in those places, namely, the formation of broad strips of transport materials that constitute the superficial and frontal moraines of the glacier.

First picture of Glacier San Quintin to the left and right of the hill (Cerro (Co) Yañez) in the middle[06]

Following the indications of the South American Pilot, we look for - after having entered the estuary - the north coast that presents formidable ravines of rocks cut to the ground and covered with thick vegetation. We follow the channel between this coast and a high island, carefully probing, to avoid low ones that can be seen near the western end of the island and further on in the interior of the estuary. As on other occasions, we noticed some difference between our soundings and those indicated by the English chart. At points, for example, where the chart indicates/marks 20 and 10 fathoms, we measure 30 and more, without finding a bottom. Finally, we anchor in 25 fathoms facing the northwest end of the island mentioned above.

When wind and rain had been calmed down, we took advantage of the afternoon of the same day 12, to recce the interior of the estuary and the rivers that flow to it. During navigation in the Gulf of San Esteban we had seen three main inlets that terminate in the contours of the estuary: one to the south that branches through the mountain ranges next to the coast; another one inland that descends from the SE. at the western foot of a sugar-loaf-shaped mountain, and the third that finishes at the eastern end of the estuary, revealing, like the second, powerful masses of ice at its backdrop. As only the last two could be the object of our reconnaissance, I commissioned Messrs. Michell and Count Schulenburg for the studies of the southern coast, to seek entry into a river that comes out of the inlet of the SE. in between lows and flat marshes, while Mr. Humbleton and I moved into the estuary.

The first party had great difficulty to find an accessible channel of the river, having to pass a bar with dangerous surf. It was found that the river, despite its width of about 100 meters, comes only from one tongue of the glacier that can be seen at close range, behind the back of the mentioned sugar bread mountain. At its mouth a delta forms, whose greater arm is the one that comes out more towards the west and whose mouth goes up around the high island by the west. It seems that the flood plains that stay dry at low tide, extend throughout the intermediary space between the island and the continent. The river takes along pieces of ice that can be seen scattered throughout the length of its bed.

The navigation in the eastern part of the estuary is very difficult because of the shallows that emerge from some points on the southern side and traverse almost the entire width of the bay. On the north coast, the wall of mountains continues, with inaccessible ravines, whose monotony is interrupted only by a magnificent waterfall that rushes with a powerful gush of yellowish-brown water into a small cove. We have noticed that such a colour is particular to all the rivers and streams of this region that are formed from springs or ponds in the middle of the bush, especially in the very thick *Laureliopsis philippiana* forests[31] that dominate the vegetation, replacing the Quila[32] scrubs that disappear to the south of the isthmus of Ofqui. To reach the far east of the bay, we followed with great work a channel, whose ramifications between the shallows were indicated by the outflowing tide.

We have constantly seen a great wall of ice that extends from north to south, closing the entire width of the eastern extension of the inlet that is below of it. Its connection with the glacier spotted at the inside of the SE inlet is evident, so that the estuary Kelly is surrounded in a semi-circular way and a short distance from the coast, by a real amphitheatre of glaciers that emanate from a vast snow-covered field, visible between peaks of the mountain ranges on the distant eastern horizon.

On the other hand, we have not been able to discover the point of the glacier that according to the maps of Fitzroy [21] and Simpson, ends in the inner part of the north side of the estuary Kelly. As we passed by this place, we saw only the uninterrupted continuation of a high mountain covered in its peaks of mosses and rickety vegetation, and in its lower slopes a bush entangled with tepa[33], Patagonian oak[34], *Pilgerodendron uviferum*[35], etc. Towards the interior, the mountain continues bordering the eastern inlet and is cut by two or three smaller inlets that come down from the north, set before the great depression where the glacier opens up its road, whose distance from the beach in this part should not be less than from 6 to 7 miles. The geological habit of the hills of the northern band is old plutonic. A rock taken from the cliffs at the foot of the waterfall, turned out to be a diabase[36], which crosses strata of ancient schites (amphibolites[37]?) whose samples can be seen in the naked ravines of the sugar loaf mountain.

The intermediary space between the eastern end of the estuary and the ice barrier of the glacier is occupied by a wide plain covered with forest, mainly *Pilgerodendron uviferum*[38]. The branches of a medium sized river cross it; but our attempt to get upriver in the shallop failed after having travelled a short distance, the cause were the barricades of sticks and logs that obstruct the passage. More upriver, a broadening of the river in the form of a lagoon is discovered, and it is evident that its origin is only in the brooks from the glacier and the streams from the smaller coves that unite in different parts of the plains.

Summed up, the conditions offered by the Kelly estuary as a starting point towards the interior of the mountain ranges are the worst that can be imagined. It does not give access to any valley of a navigable river by boat, and even the march by land would soon end at the foot of the ice ravines, not counting the impediment of the forest and muddy and flooded terrain that fills the inferior and accessible part of the inlet. In the contours of the estuary steep mountain cliffs predominate, and the few tracts of low ground are useless, for being exposed to the avenues of the rivers fed by the melting of powerful glaciers.

Very similar was the result that we obtained from the reconnaissance in the estuary of the Jesuits, explored on the 13th to the 15th of December.

Having left the mouth of the estuary Kelly, we took course SSE. to pass through the wide channel that separates the continental coast from the high and ravine massif of the island of San Javier.

Steffen included the following relevant notes:

[20]   At the exit of the bay we were convinced that the rocky island marked on the maps of Fitzroy and Simpson with the name of 'Island of the Surgeon', has been transformed into a peninsula, united with the Forelius by an isthmus covered with trees . This is one of the many cases that indicate oscillations in the littoral of the Chilean Patagonia in historical times.

[21]   See the sketch inserted in Darwin's work, 'Journal of Researches,' etc. (London 1840), page 285.

Another documented activity occurred in the Istmo de Ofqui before the 1920/21 expedition. This activity was to explore the

Istmo de Ofqui scientifically in order to search for a way to create a route for vessels across the isthmus to enable small vessels to travel safely from north to south and avoid the treacherous seas around Cabo Raper. This activity started in 1905 and continued until 1908. It also included many detailed surveys of the south coast of the Taitao Peninsula to see if there were any other possible routes using some of the many other lakes that are common in this region.

Amazingly, Golfo de Penas, and more specifically Bahia San Quintin, had a role to play in World War 1. Commander Stokes of HMS *Beagle* would not have realised the significance of his statement that "if Saint Quintin's Sound or Inlet were situated in quarter of the world where the advantages it offers to shipping might be profited by, it would be deemed a fine spacious and secured Harbour". When repeated in the *Admiralty Pilot*, this provided the German East Asia Squadron[39], consisting of *Scharnhorst, Gneisenau, Leipzig, Nürnberg* and *Dresden*, a safe haven to re-coal ships and relax away from prying eyes between two tragic sea battles, the Battle of Coronel and the Battle of the Falkland Islands. At the Battle of Coronel on 1st November 1914, the German squadron under the command of Vice Admiral Graf von Spee defeated the British squadron and sank HMS *Good Hope* and HMS *Monmouth* with the loss of 1,600 lives. Chile was a neutral country so belligerents could only stay in port for 24 hours.

After the battle, the German admiral needed to get his ships back to Germany via Cape Horn, so after taking on coal at Más Afuera from a collier, the squadron anchored at Bahia San Quintin (Map of Golfo de Penas – Route 7). One wonders if the squadron was spotted by the staff at the new lighthouse at Cabo Raper[40] as they sailed by. Arriving in the gulf on 21st November, they anchored, met up with their seven colliers and filled all five warships with so much coal that it was stacked on the upper deck. By all accounts, the weather was calm during their stay and sailors went ashore to cut Christmas trees. The kaiser signalled that he was awarding von Spee the Iron Cross, First Class and von Spee was to award 300 Iron Crosses, Second Class to the crews of the squadron ships. The admiral went from ship to ship, naming and congratulating the recipients (although the medals themselves waited in Germany for the squadron's return). After being able to relax for a few days, the squadron sailed south into the Pacific and mountainous seas on 26th November. On 8th December 1914, four ships of the German East Asia Squadron were sunk by a stronger British force off the Falkland Islands; only the *Dresden* escaped. Nearly 2,000 German sailors lost their lives.

The stage was then set for Professor Otto Nordenskjold's 1920/21 Swedish expedition to South America and Chilean Patagonia in particular (Map of Golfo de Penas – Route 8).

Chapter 1

THE 1920/21 SWEDISH EXPEDITION TO CHILEAN PATAGONIA – THE PLAN AND PARTICIPANTS

Compiled by Martin Sessions except where indicated otherwise

Professor Otto Nordenskjöld

Professor Otto Nordenskjöld (the Professor or Prof in this story) was a remarkable explorer and scientist[01].

Professor Nordenskjöld at Kelly Inlet

He was born on 6th December 1869 on the estate Sjögle, Mariannelund, Småland in Sweden. His father, Gustaf Nordenskjöld, was an army captain, whilst his mother Anna, born Nordenskiöld, was the sister of the polar explorer Adolf Erik Nordenskiöld.

Studying at Uppsala University from 1886, he obtained his doctorate in geology in 1894. Soon after he led his first major expedition to Tierra del Fuego in 1895 and then went on to explore the southern mountains of Patagonia where the Cordillera of the Andes is interpenetrated by the fjords of the Pacific[02]. In particular, he demonstrated that the watershed was not related to the Cordillera as the watershed was to be boundary between Chile and Argentina.

In 1898, he conducted a small scientific expedition to the Klondyke region of Canada.

Interest by many countries in Antarctic exploration was gaining momentum and Otto Nordenskjöld was determined that Sweden should also take part in Antarctic research. He started to raise funds by private and public appeals for the Antarctic expedition. Also, he added to his experience by going to Scoresbysund, East Greenland, as the geologist of C G Amdrup's expedition in 1900. On the way back from this expedition, he met his future wife, Karen Berg, who was living in Dyrafjord, Iceland.

He secured a ship, named *Antarctic*, and an experienced polar captain, Captain C A Larsen. With a team of able assistants, he reached his base in the Weddel Sea early in the Antarctic summer of 1901-02 at Snow Hill Island. Two other expeditions were in the Antarctic that summer, the *Gauss* under Professor E von Drygalski and *Discovery* under Captain R Scott, RN but only the Swedish expedition overwintered. The *Antarctic* failed to return to pick them up in the summer of 1902-03; the ship was crushed by the ice of the Weddel Sea and the expedition was now split into three parties who all overwintered for the second year. Amazingly all three parties met up in the summer of 1903-04 to be 'rescued' by the Argentine vessel, the *Uruguay*. All but one of the 24-strong team returned to Sweden bringing with them an incredible collection of data, in particular meteorological observations, and samples including invaluable palaeontology samples[03].

On his return to Europe, he was appointed professor of geography and ethnography at the University of Gothenburg. Together with writing a mammoth report of the results of his expedition, he also set his heart on returning to the Antarctic a second time to resolve the many questions connected with polar geography, glaciology and geology. By 1913, he had developed a plan and organised support for an Anglo-Swedish expedition, but the Great War put that plan on hold.

He undertook further exploration on the west coast of Greenland in 1909.

The Plan

The plan for the 1920/21 Swedish expedition to South America (Chilean Patagonia phase) is best described by Professor Otto Nordenskjöld's summary of the expedition in a lecture to the Swedish Society for Anthropology and Geography on 18th November 1921[04].

Swedish science knew little about South America in 1897 but a Swedish shipping company, the Johnson Line, trading with South America, transported many scientists to study this continent in the following years.

Nordenskjöld goes on to say, 'However, from the collected funds, the committee, which had in its hand the leadership of the South Pole Expedition, made a sum at its disposal

for a trip to South America'. General Consul Axel Axelson
Johnson granted the expedition free journeys and shipping
in the line's vessels, and also made a direct financial con-
tribution. Professor LA Jägerskiöld raised a sum to allow
a zoologist, Count Sten von Rosen, to accompany and collect collections for the Gothenburg Museum. The other two
members of the expedition, Allan Bäckman 'student' and
'Patagonian' Captain H N Pallin raised the funds needed
for their participation. Nordenskjöld, Bäckman and Rosen
travelled from Gothenburg at the beginning of 1920 for
an expedition in Peru first whilst Pallin arrived in Chile in
November 1920.

Time for the expedition was very limited for several reasons.
He says:

My plan was for a purely geographic research expedition; how
tempting it could be, we must refrain from immersing ourselves
in the detail work and instead make sure we see as much of
the country as possible; look and compare and study to seek a
clearer view of nature and cultural conditions, just this, which is
now increasingly emerging as the goal and content of scientific
geography. To achieve this, we need to visit some of the most
important cultural centres, cities and the most important business geographic centres, but also some of the most unknown,
hardest available areas, where we could hope to make new contributions to understanding South American nature. As my first
goal, I had made a visit to the ancient wonderful fairy tale of
Peru with its strange history and with a nature that might out-
weigh anything else the earth could offer in such a limited space.
No country should offer greater attractions to a researcher, and
never before had any Swedish natural science expedition worked
in Peru.

The second part of the expedition was to be to the Patagonian region of Chile. He describes this part of the plan as follows:

What gives this region (the South Patagonian high-mountain areas) such an interest is the mighty ice mass which, in relation to its position at the latitude of central France, is unique on the earth, covering those mountains and sending down their 'runners' to or near the sea level. In my first trip, I was on one of those eastward from the earliest reaches to these glaciers, later having their peripheral areas from both the west and the east is also welcomed by Swedish expeditions, Skottsberg and Quensel, and an Argentine-German expedition is even far down in the south-east penetrated into the ice, but no one has tried to study this closer, and in the whole of the northern part of this vast icefield, which as a unit has a length of at least 6 latitudes, 700 kilometres, almost none of us had ever been at the edge of the ice. And whoever knows what the obstacles nature places here, can understand the reasons for this. For the whole understanding of the ice age in the southern hemisphere, however, it should be of particular interest to get to know this ice, which is still in the newest literature, often called the 'Patagonian ice sheet', to know its form and extent, the changes in its propagation and conditions for its origin at this low latitude.

An expedition, which does not have its own ships, has to reach this region, relying on the will of the Chilean Government. The Swedish Minister Hultgren had already made a resignation to us to help us with our trip down there, and despite major internal difficulties, economic depression and coal strikes, we were received in Chile with the utmost goodwill and immediately got permission to accompany a ship, which went out to supply the Patagonian lighthouses, and to land at the place we wanted to designate, and then on the agreed time there to be picked up. But it was about finding the right place, because once you were there, you got to be there, and in an unfortunate case you could risk that nothing was done at all. About 46 1/2° south lies the widely known San Rafael glacier, which, from a narrow valley, sprouts outwards in an almost circular fan, calving ice filled lake. Even slightly more south, there is a much larger ice stream, the San Tadeo glacier, whose shimmering white mass can be seen far out at sea, but never reached by any expedition, which was unknown both to its origin and its end, although it was believed to assume that its tongue reached a somewhat inaccessible swamp. Directly reaching from the front must therefore be considered very difficult, but I decided to try a flank attack. Just south of the San Tadeo glacier, in parallel with this, the powerful Gulf of Penas enters the little Kelly Fjord, 'one of the most desolate and wildest places on this deserted coast', as it is called in the *Beagle* expedition's work. Here, however, one should be able to find a sheltered place where our equipment could be landed, and from here I wanted to try crossing the mountain ridge to the edge of the ice. Had we been lucky we might have here at a higher altitude find smoother ice, which did not produce too many big obstacles in the way of a long ice hike.

The Other Participants

Hugo Nikolaus (Nils) Pallin, H N Pallin, was a civil engineer, an explorer and a mountaineer. He was born 5th of April 1880 in Gävle[05], Sweden. His mother died when he was very young and the family moved to Stockholm a few years later.

He left school in 1897 to start working as an apprentice in a small engineering company while planning to be a sailor and see the world. He eventually went to sea but returned home to Stockholm in 1898 where he attended and graduated from an upper secondary school of technology in 1900. He then went on to study at the Royal Institute of Technology (Kungl.

Tekniska högskolan), from where he graduated in 1904 as a civil engineer, and in 1905 also as an officer in the Road and Water Construction Service Corps of the Army.

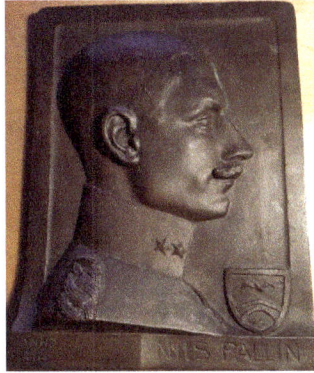

Lieutenant H N Pallin in 1911[06]

He was a hardworking man with wide-ranging interests. He was assistant engineer at the Central Road and Waterfront District and from 1905 to 1907 also at the National Swedish Road Board. He studied at the Sorbonne University Paris in 1908, and worked as an engineer in the construction of the subway in Paris between 1908 and 1909.

He became lieutenant in the Road and Water Construction Service Corps in 1910. Between 1910 and 1911 he was an assistant to the Stockholm City Construction Manager. From 1912 he continued working as first office engineer, office manager and district engineer at the National Swedish Road Board, and in various Swedish districts. He served as consultant engineer in communications and planning issues from 1910, as secretary of the Stockholm Civil Aviation Administration in 1920, member of the Board of Directors in 1917.

He was one of the founders of De lappländska fjällkarlarnas klubb (The Laponic Mountain Men's Club, a club for mountaineering enthusiasts, which existed from 1920-1973 when the last member died). He made the first winter ascent of Kebnekaise (1908), Sarektjåkko (1916) and Kaskasatjåkko (1920).

His numerous writings up to the start of the expedition in 1920 mostly dealt with traffic questions and questions of the construction of roads and bridges, and were written in Swedish.

At the start of the expedition, he was 40.

Sten von Rosen was a biologist and explorer[07]. On the expedition he was to be the zoologist. He was born 14 July 1897 in Stockholm and baptized as Sten Adalbert Ottokar Horn von Rosen. His father was Reinhold Gustaf Edvard von Rosen Moore and his mother was Elsa Vilhelmina Agneta Sofia Florence von Rosen (nee Horn). He graduated from 'Gymnasiet' (high school) in 1917, studied at 'Högskola' (college) in Stockholm and at the University in Wien. He accompanied Professor Otto Nordenskjöld firstly to Peru before commencing the second phase of the expedition when he was 23.

Sten von Rosen in Peru

Allan Bäckman was born on the island Visingsö 5th March 1893, located in Sweden's second largest sea 'Vättern'[08]. He was baptized as Tor Allan Bäckman. His father was Carl

Oscar Bäckman and his mother Johanna Sofia Bäckman (nee Svenningsdotter). He graduated from 'Gymnasium' (high school) in 1911 and went on to become a school teacher in 1914. He accompanied Professor Otto Nordenskjöld firstly to Peru before commencing the second phase of the expedition when he was 27. Whilst in Peru, he contracted malaria but had recovered for the second part of the expedition. He was the expedition's 'geographer' and meteorologist.

Allan Bäckman in Peru

Pedro, Liborio and Oligari were three Chilotes (inhabitants of Chiloe) who were hired from Queilén on the island of Chiloe to provide assistance especially in the roles of creating routes over the mountain range and to Glacier Andreé and transporting expedition stores. There are few photographs of them and very little other information other than what Allan has included in his letters home. 'They were willing and helpful, did not budge, were happy and content in the most devilish conditions. Pedro and Liborio in particular were magnificent individuals. If you watched Oligari, he would assist too.'

✧

Chapter 2

ADVENTURES IN PATAGONIA

by Nils Pallin[01]

The expedition team onboard the Yañez *with Captain Merino are Nils Pallin, Professor Otto Nordenskjöld and Allan Bäckman*

When our expeditions among the Arauca Indians were completed, Professor Nordenskjöld and I departed in early December 1920 from Temuco further south to Puerto Montt.

We united with our colleagues to finish the preparations for the voyage to Patagonia, the main goal of our trip.

From Temuco the open and fertile Indian landscape extends around this town some twenty kilometres to the south. From there the country gradually begins to fold, and large forests cover its surface, in many places burnt down for colonization. The bare trunks blackened by fire, in long lines stretching their hands towards the sky, are like a desperate accusation against man's never-ending devastation of nature. The various coastal ridges of the Cordilleras unite here in the neighbourhood of Puerto Montt to dive down under the sea. Then with renewed vigour they reemerge, first in the large island of Chiloé and then in the towering, extremely shattered archipelago, with innumerable channels and fjords, along the entire coast of West Patagonia.

Large and fertile plains opened at Antilhue where the railway to Valdivia takes off. It is in these districts that the German emigration made such beautiful conquests. In Osorno we spent the night in the town hotel. It was overcrowded (to say the least) as a result of an agricultural exhibition. The next day we passed by the beautiful lake Llanquihue with its wide waters and snow covered, easily accessible mountains which has provided the area with the name 'Chilean Switzerland', and further up to Puerto Montt, where the railway network has its terminus[02].

Puerto Montt is located on the large bay Golfo de Ancud, inside of Chiloé, at the southern end of central Chile. The strip of land that remains between the southern end of the Cordilleras and the ocean is so torn, mountainous and narrow, and also so moist, that only a very small population has found its livelihood there, and this only in the area closest to Puerto Montt. This small town, which has no more than 6,000 inhabitants, is already very rainy. However, there are also beautiful days especially in the summer. The climate is of a pronounced humid type, and the further you get towards the south the greater the amount of rainfall.

Puerto Montt in 1920

Puerto Montt is otherwise a nice little town during the summer season. It was even more so during our visit, when several warships lay at anchor because of the celebration of the three hundred years memorial of Magellan's feat, and with life and colour everywhere.

There, however, we stayed no longer than necessary. Already after three days, the little Government steamer *Yañez* was ready to go, and we had finished our preparations. Previously I described the gracious attention that was shown to us everywhere in Chile. Unfortunately, this attention now spread to the less honourable thief trade. The luggage consignment by boat from Valparaiso to Puerto Montt had been broken in to and the contents of my chief equipment trunk stolen. According to provided information, about twenty percent of all transit goods in Chile get stolen, and if one is hit by these percentages, the other portion goes free. You had to be glad that nothing more was stolen. After all, while it may be sad to have your many years of good companionship with a pair of old, very nice trousers interrupted for the future, it would have been worse to have a leg broken. So, with the wallet in your fist, it was only to visit the major department store in Puerto Montt and replace the stolen items, as far as was possible. In fairness it should be added, that after my return to Valparaiso and through the mediation of the Swedish Consul General (the Irishman JJ Heavy), I received a thousand pesos in indemnification from the shipping company Brown & Blanchard in Punta Arenas. This was rare for South American conditions, and certainly could be attributed to the nationality of the expedition and appreciation of its importance to Chile.

The Yañez[03]. *Expedition members were in the deckhouse at the stern*

Another government steamer in Puerto Montt, the *Elicura,* was significantly newer and larger than *Yañez*. By complaisance of the commander, we were able to travel with *Elicura* during the first day. On the evening of Saturday, 11th December 1920, after experiencing a quite noticeable earthquake, we boarded from the pier in Puerto Montt, and at 4 am the following morning we cleared anchor to leave for our chosen landing site in the Kelly Fjord[04]. The course was first set at Queilén, a small town on the east side of the island of Chiloe, where we went in to hire the men needed for the expedition. These were three Chilotes[05] named Livorio, Pedro and Olegari, who came aboard with their sacks the next day.

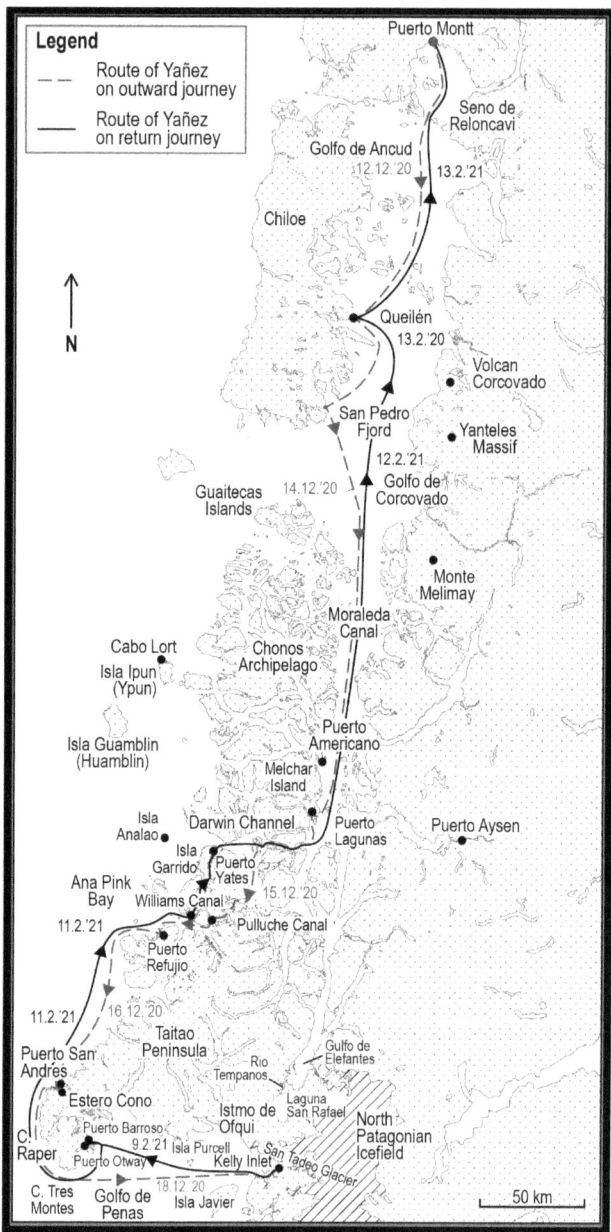

Legend

— — Route of Yañez
       on outward journey

——— Route of Yañez
       on return journey

Puerto Montt

Seno de
Reloncavi

Golfo de Ancud
12.12.'20   13.2.'21

Chiloe

N

Queilén
13.2.'20

Volcan
Corcovado

San Pedro
Fjord

Yanteles
Massif

12.2.'21

Guaitecas   14.12.'20   Golfo de
Islands   Corcovado

Monte
Melimay

Moraleda
Canal

Cabo Lort   Chonos
Isla Ipun   Archipelago
(Ypun)

Puerto
Americano

Isla Guamblin
(Huamblin)

Melchar
Island

Isla   Darwin Channel   Puerto   Puerto Aysen
Analao   Lagunas
              Isla
Ana Pink   Garrido   Puerto
Bay   Yates
         Williams Canal 15.12.'20
11.2.'21
                          Pulluche Canal
         Puerto
         Refujio

11.2.'21   16.12.'20
              Taitao
Puerto San   Peninsula   Rio   Gulfo de
Andrés   Tempanos   Elefantes

Estero Cono   Istmo de   Laguna
                          Ofqui   San Rafael   North
C.   Puerto Barroso   Patagonian
Raper   Puerto Otway 9.2.'21 Isla Purcell San Icefield
                              Kelly Inlet Tadeo Glacier
C. Tres   Golfo de 18.12.'20
Montes   Penas   Isla Javier   50 km

Map of routes taken by Yañez *to support the expedition*

Is this Queilén in December 1920?

During the stay in Queilén, we went on a little riding tour into the island to get the opportunity to see some Chilote farms and to study the 'feared' vegetation, which begins to develop here, in preparation for South Patagonia. Chiloé is about as large as Gotland [the largest Swedish island], and occupied almost exclusively by the Chilotes, a fairly pure, indigenous population of Indian origin. Their main food is fish and potatoes; they are good sailors and modest men. Our guide on the ride was one of these locals. While we were on horseback, he followed us on foot, mostly running.

We followed a road, which ran along the coast at the desolate edge of vertical beach cliffs, in some places more than a hundred metres high. At the bottom of which the sea rushed mightily towards the beach which was covered by crabs and seaweed. After a few hours ride we were in the Chilotes inhabited landscape, where we visited two farms and were given an opportunity to see their simple sheds, strange kitchen houses or summer farms, and characteristic thatched roof cattle corrals. We did also experience a lot of interesting vegetation during the ride, which on the way back was made through rain.

A Chiloé farm scene

After returning to *Yañez*, anchors were weighed, and we steamed south, passing islands cultivated in patches, and coasts, to the San Pedro Fjord on the south side of Chiloé where we anchored for the night.

The following morning, we sailed out into the Gulf of Corcovado in a gloomy mist, which gradually lightened into one of the most beautiful days that God had ever let shine over this residence of rain. It was so much more gratifying because we were now able to see the magnificent gulf with its amazing coast of ice and volcanoes. To the north lay 'The famous Corcovado', an extinct volcano, whose tip is so sharp that you nearly feel hurt when you look at it. After this, to the south follows the mighty Yanteles massif and to the south rises the white dressed volcano Melimoyu, whose two horns give the mountain the appearance of a snail. Over the lustrous waters, penguins were rushing to escape, and fur seals were sunbathing on the bare rocks.

Yanteles Massif in the centre

From the Gulf of Corcovado, our course was straight south through the wide Moraleda Canal, in the length of which the sky and the sea appear to converge. To the west, between this channel and the Pacific Ocean, is the rough-cut Chonos Archipelago. On the map, this has the appearance of a giant mirror, which has been crushed by falling objects, forming channels between the immense shards. When you see its orography, you are struck by the resemblance of clay, cracked by solidifying. Searching to explain their formation without profundity, you cannot avoid finding the explanation that underground pressure made the rock crust burst.

This evening we anchored in the small bay of Puerto Lagunas on Melchor Island to continue our journey to the south the following morning.

The Chilean archipelago has a variety of excellent fairways in the wide and deep 'canals' between the islands. All the way from Puerto Montt to Punta Arenas of Magellan sound - i.e., a distance of more than 1,500 kilometres - you can travel through these inshore water ways. This is a very big advantage, since the ocean outside is beset generally by strong winds and heavy seas. Only in one place you have to go out to sea. That is to pass the Taitao Peninsula, which through the narrow and low Ofqui Isthmus is connected with the continent, and from there extends all the way out to the open sea shore. It is a nasty passage for all ships, but especially for small boats. A possible channel through the isthmus of the many fjords into the peninsula has long been sought but in vain. The Chilean government then equipped an expedition and set up a proposal for a canal through the Ofqui Isthmus. This commission delivered its geographically very interesting report in 1909.

The isthmus which connects the Taitao Peninsula with the mainland is low and swampy, and is obviously the remains of a centuries-old firth, which has been filled up by deposition of materials from the still active glaciers close to the coast. In the middle of the isthmus lies the famous glacier lake Laguna San Rafael, in which the Rafael Glacier starting from the east ends with a huge, fan-shaped ice ridge. The lake is connected to the sea by the north flowing, and into the Golfo de Elefantes, Rio Tempanos (the ice block river), through which the tide moves the glacier ice blocks back and forth from the lake which has the same water level as the sea.

The river is navigable for quite large vessels up to the lake, but from Laguna San Rafael to the sea bay of Golfo de Penas south of the peninsula, a canal must cut through a distance of two kilometres of the so-called 'genuine Ofqui Isthmus'. The other, 'ungenuine' part of the isthmus is already cut through by the Rio Tempanos. This new, dug-out section of the canal should have a depth below the low tide of five metres and a bottom width of twenty metres. If it should be built, it would make a considerable improvement in maritime conditions on the west coast of South America. In the south part of its run, the planned canal would follow Rio San Tadeo, which for a large part is fed from the enormous San Tadeo Glacier[06], just south of the Rafael Glacier and the goal of our expedition.

The San Tadeo River leads into Bahia San Quintin, on the inside of the Peninsula Forelius (Note 1 in Chapter 7), which forms part of the south coast of the Taitao Peninsula, towards the Golfo de Penas. The entire peninsula is incredibly swampy and bushy, cut through as it is by the countless arms of glacial rivers and covered by primeval forests, which in large areas are dead - a still partly unexplained phenomena. From everyone who visited these areas for centuries-long lamentations have been heard, about the indescribably rainy and heinous climate, which by the way was close to making the work of the Ofqui Commission impossible. It has also been suggested to place a penal colony here for the purpose of building the canal[07].

Chonos Archipelago scenery

From Puerto Lagunas on 15th December, we steered west-wards into the Darwin Channel and further in south-western direction through several narrow canals out onto the open sea to bypass the Taitao. The weather was stormy and rainy grey, and hence we could not fully enjoy the magnificent fjord scenery that in many ways is reminiscent of Norway. Already at the end of the Darwin Channel we were given a presentiment of the ocean, whose waves fell in over us from the side, through a narrow inlet that this channel opens to the seaside. But it got worse when in the evening we approached the open sea, to cast anchor for the night in the small fjord Puerto Refugio, whose mouth is directly facing the ocean. At the end of Wickham mouth, we had a rough head sea, and the small *Yañez*, that was almost reminiscent of a big tug, worked fiercely in the waves. Out in Ana Pink Bay[08], it was dreadful to see the rolling sea, with greyish black rain squalls, and the naked rocks whose contours barely could be seen through the late evening. Every sound was drowned by the whistling storm and the thundering bass drum of the surfs. The rain stood spraying as billowing fields of corn between the clouds and the sea. It was a light-hearted moment, when we could let our storm anchor go in the reasonably protected Refugio Bay.

More Chonos Archipelago scenery

On these coasts no human being lives. The Chilotes occasionally intervene here in their search for otters (nutria)[09] and in the waters south of the Taitao Peninsula there are still some sparse groups of canal Indians, who nevertheless never venture across the Golfo de Penas. Except from those, the whole of West Patagonia is virtually uninhabited, except for close to Magellan's Inlet. Puerto Refugio was consequently just as deserted as the San Pedro and Lagunas had previously been. All three of them as well as the other channel harbours were only natural ones without a trace of human intervention. The following day, when it was still unthinkable to go out to the sea because of the bad weather, we were accompanied by a small coastal steamer *Huandad* that also sought refuge in Refugio from the storm.

The Huandad

There was a pleasant interruption in the bad weather. Between the rain showers we were invited to a clam feast on the shore by the captain and the passengers on the ship. They had been in Puerto Americano the previous night, a channel port which is known for its rich supply of choros. A choros is a blue clam (*Mytilus edulis*) about fifteen centimetres long which can be used for cooking 'curanto'. This was made by setting up a fire under the trees on the beach, to heat the stony ground properly. Then the fire and the ashes were scrabbled away. Then the mussels, which were kept alive as oysters in sacks, were poured out over the rocks. Over the mussels were put raw potatoes and fresh ferns, then pancakes, and new ferns, then a mutton shoulder and new ferns. The pile was covered with wet sacks, turf and stones. It was then allowed to stand and get roasted for half an hour, after which the layers were removed in reverse order. The dish tasted good, although an inexperienced consumer will in the long run get tired of all the molluscs, he is forced to make acquaintance with in these districts. Beer, wine and cigarettes were served with the meal, and after its finish some participating girls sang a couple of moving Chilean songs. Their dark beauty and bright voices formed a strange element from a distant world of feeling in this wasteland, whose harsh and shivery temper otherwise appeared to rule out any trace of weakness.

Preparing the 'curanto'

The following morning at half-past four both *Yañez* and *Huandad* weighed anchors, and after a quarter of an hour we were out on the foaming ocean. The poor *Yañez* was flung like a toy between mountains of grey water, over which she flew like a chip. *Huandad* immediately disappeared out of sight behind us. I hardly believed that you could make it with such a small ship as *Yañez* in such a seaway. But the Chilean Navy men are accustomed to the terrible sea in the south, to which its officers significantly are appointed no more than six months at a time. And still they have a saying, that every such period makes them three years older.

It was impossible to frequent the deck. The four members of the expedition who had the disposal of a small deckhouse near the stern, had to stay inside it with the risk that the entire house could be washed overboard by the first strong surge. We went close to the shore, where the high cone formed mountains ended in plain coastal rocks. In some places, these were scattered into sharp rocks over which the Earth's

A magnificent bare rockface

most magnificent surge sprayed its sky high froth. Over this rushing world hovered majestic albatrosses in quiet comfort, immense gulls with wings so large that they could give rise to the legend about the birds with wings that reached around the world.

Woe is the seafarer who gets into distress on this coast. He can be likened to a man who falls from an airplane. Nine out of ten times, he is lost. And this was also very close to become the fate of the expedition. We had been offshore for six hours, when we observed that the engine was starting to run slowly. It is a bad sign if you slow down in troubled waters and even more on an unclean coast. The others didn't cling to it, but I lay in my hammock listening, and not without worry. For more than one hour we went with this speed. The boat was thrown so violently in the surge that the swinging hammock in which I lay first broke the thick ceiling lamp column, and then swung all the way up to the roof of the deckhouse. Finally the engine began to increase the pace, and we could again indulge in our arduous fantasies in the lulling noise from the rattle and roar of the water on deck. To sleep was impossible. A drowsy half sleep was everything that occasionally was possible. We had a long day in front of us, as the passage around Taitao Peninsula often takes a day. We were therefore very surprised, when already at one o'clock p.m. we suddenly steered forward into calm waters and in slow speed reached a sheltered spot where the anchor was dropped.

The captain now came to the stern and informed us about the context. A severe engine damage had occurred in the open sea. I think it was the packing-box for the slide that had been loosened by the hard waves against the boat. The slide bar had bent and rendered the machine unusable, in the middle of the worst storm. By a masterstroke, the engineer had managed to keep the machine running by manual strength until he had time to provisionally repair the damage. After which

Captain Merino

Professor Nordenskjöld thinking about the challenges ahead

the captain made our way into the small emergency port of San Andres where we now lay. I later went down to the engine and inspected the damage and was able to fully identify the serious danger we had been in. However, the whole trip had been so raw and shivery that we only thought of continuing. Captain Merino wrote me a letter a year later in which he stated that in fact he had never let us know how close to the grave we had been.

We spent the rest of the day in the idyllically beautiful San Andres, also called Puerto Cono, and the following day, too, to repair the engine. The place is famous for its good fishing. The men embarked on a fishing trip and came back aboard with 48 robalos, a whitefish-looking fish, which tasted excellent.

But the rain was pouring down in streams, and everything was dripping wet. I started to understand why the Patagonian Indians go nearly plain naked, despite the eternal rain and the cold which often drops below freezing point. It is quite simply the only way to avoid the wet clothes, and it is very possible that this practice is to be seen as one of the strangest adaptations to an extreme climate. I presented this maybe somewhat facile theory in an interview in a Valparaiso paper a few months afterwards, and it seemed to win a fashionable appreciation.

After the engine had been tested the following morning, we again made our way out into the now less rough sea. Not long afterwards we passed Cabo Raper[10], where one of the few lighthouses on the Patagonian coast is located. A little later we passed Cabo Tres Montes, where you turn to the east into the Golfo de Penas, after finally having rounded the Taitao Peninsula.

Golfo de Penas is justly bearing the name 'Bay of Trouble', for it is open like the sea and its coasts are known for their furious surf. We headed from Cabo Tres Montes in straight easterly course to Kelly Fjord [Kelly Inlet] in whose interior parts we should disembark. Through immense crowds of seabirds, we approached the rainy coast along the Forelius Peninsula (named after a Swede, Note 1 in Chapter 7). On the inside is one of the world's best natural roadsteads, with room for all the naval fleets of the world. To starboard we had the island of San Javier, a rock fragment from the Coast Cordilleras, but which had been left alone out in the gulf. From there, we caught the first glance of ice of the Tadeo Glacier. It began to gleam like a white ghost through the grey fog, showing its blurry masses of ice, which are among the largest on earth.

View from Golfo de Penas approaching Kelly Inlet on the right wrapped in grey mist.
On the left is Glacier San Tadeo (San Quintin)[11]

Around five o'clock in the evening we steamed with thrill out into the fog and rain-soaked Kelly Fjord. Its first modern visitor, Fitz-Roy, a century earlier had stated, that it is one of the bleakest and most inhospitable places in this deserted coast[12]. Its contours hardly fit with the maps. Gently sounding, we were searching ourselves inwards to find an anchorage. Just before six in the evening a soft shock was felt, and we were stuck in the bottom clay. As it was high tide, the grounding was unpleasant, and it was hard work for the commander and crew to remove the ship from its tough mooring. After long reversing and warping, the ship was eventually afloat around eight o'clock in the evening. This happy event was celebrated with a bottle of dry

champagne - a gift to the expedition from the Swedish Minister
Claes Hultgren in Buenos Aires and Santiago.

Yañez *at anchor in Kelly Inlet – note the mist*

The following morning our disembarkation started, preceded
by a reconnaissance over the sludge banks created from glacier
rock flour in the very shallow fjord. A high waterfall from the
north overthrew its rich swell. Only with difficulty you could
pass in a narrow tidal channel along this beach, and even more
difficult was it to find a suitable campsite. Fjord walls toppled
mostly steep down into the water, without leaving a place at the
beach. They gave foothold on some sparsely given beach bank,
so cluttered with primeval forest that it was practically almost
impossible to organize a camp there.

After a long search we found a landing further away into
the fjord, at a small, beautiful bay on the north side. With its
low beaches it appeared possible to clear a place for our tents.
Our luggage was transferred there and our tents were put up,
after we had created enough flat ground to get room for them
by sculpturing the actual terrain. All of this was done in the
usual pouring rain. We then returned on board. The following

Disembarking from the Yañez *in Kelly Inlet*

morning at six o'clock we left the ship in our own ship's boat
with the last pieces of luggage. The *Yañez* weighed anchor and
steamed out of the fjord, saluting us with the steam whistle. We
were now left to our fate, until we would be picked up again in
February the following year (1921). During this time, we were
to try to solve some of the most interesting problems that glaciology knows.

View to the south-west towards the entrance to Kelly Inlet.

Extracts from Allan Bäckman's Letters[13]

Nils Pallin and Allan Bäckman on board the Yañez

Monday, 12ᵗʰ December 1920 at 8 pm. I really get to experience a lot during this journey. Imagine a tugboat of the type you have seen daily in Stockholm. Instead of the large hook in the stern, there is a cabin, 'dining room'. You probably guess the proportions. In this 'salon' we, four expedition participants, are staying together with some luggage.

The wall-mounted 40-cm-wide benches and 2 hammocks, stretched between the walls, are used as sleeping accommodation. In addition to us, the boat, including the Captain, accommodates 21 men, two families on their way out to the lighthouse at Cabo Raper, provisions for six months for this lighthouse, our luggage, which amounts to 2,000 kg, food for the crew and coal for 14 days and 45 live sheep out on the deck! The 'cargo' is in large piles everywhere. Wherever you step you put your foot in something soft! We are on our way to our work area, the mood is brilliant and the spirit of friendship is good. Now the gentlemen have gone ashore to do an hour-long horseback ride in the surroundings of Queilén. I did not follow as I have some instruments to adjust and would like to make a small profile sketch of the landscape if possible. In addition, I will take the opportunity to sleep a little, because I slept miserably in my hammock last night.

Some of the cargo on deck of the Yañez

Thursday, 15th December 1920. Today we had a wild day. The last part of yesterday, when we got out of the Pulluche Canal and Wickham Inlet, was tiring enough. A W-NW wind caused our little tug to rock violently, and I became so ill, so ill. In the end, green came in the bile. Well, I crawled, when we got into port, up in my hammock, climbed into my warm sleeping bag and fell asleep peacefully and well. Slept until 8:30. After desayuno (breakfast), the Captain, Professor, Rosen and I went ashore. We just did not get further than the beach, because the dense Patagonian primeval forest prevented us from leaving the beach strip. That forest will probably be difficult for us, when we have to go through it to get to our glacier. It is almost more difficult than the tropical primeval forest[14]. In the latter, the fallen trees rot extremely quickly, but in the Patagonia the decay takes place extremely slowly. The fallen trees, branches and twigs therefore form a layer several meters thick on the ground. Of course, it is extremely difficult to get there, especially as everything is covered with thumb-thick moss, which hides all the pits and cavities. In addition, the undergrowth is very dense and consists of a bamboo-like tube 'Quila'.

The trees are evergreen deciduous trees, beeches, etc. However, as far as I could see, they had an advantage over the trees in the tropical primeval forest, they lacked thorns. Such a trifle is valued when climbing around in the woods. The landscape, by the way, was mountainous. The steep sides, which sometimes lacked forest, fell sharply down towards the fjord. Here and there you saw a silver ribbon of a small stream, which plunged down the slopes. The peaks went up to around 900 to 1000 meters above sea level. The bedrock was mica slate with sandstone intrusions. The rolled beach gravel contained a lot of granitic and porphyritic material. Outside the fjord are some slate islands. They carry clear traces of weather and wind. Some have broken down to a few meters above the water surface, others are still so tall that they carry a small hood of shrubs and small trees on their upper part. The lower parts have been washed completely clean by the waves, which in the slate have dug beautiful small caves. I had time to draw a small profile sketch while I waited for Professor; Rosen drifted around, collected some flies, and shot a couple of birds. The Captain climbed around, most interested in Rosen's hunting, and I drifted around. At 12, a boat came and picked us up. Of course, it could not land fully, so we have to wade out to it. Soaked far up the legs. The breakfast tasted good.

18ᵗʰ December 1920 - Puerto San Andres; Cono Inlet. From Puerto Refugio, the ship left early yesterday morning. After half an hour we were out on the open sea. It was an experience! I first noticed it on the hammock's swings, which grew with each passing minute. Eventually they became so big that I pounded alternately against the wall, alternately against the lamp. It was too much. I became somewhat nauseous, climbed down and placed myself next to a bucket, which was filled as much as I was emptied. So, I needed to poo and had to go to the toilet room. Then the key was missing; I had to stand outside on the deck and wait, while the chef ran around the ship and looked for the key. Meanwhile, I was surprised by a 'tidal' wave. It came in over the shoulder, rushed through the open passage in the middle of me. I was thrown like a ball against the wall and of course became completely soaked. Finally the chef came with the key, and I could do what was needed. So, I returned to our 'salon'. It was half full of water. Every wave that came splashed a few litres into a doorway and in the end everything floated around inside. Then I heard a bang. Pallin, lying in the other hammock, had turned against the ceiling lamp, which cracked and pounded on the table. All my attempts to get up into my hammock failed. I have to sit on the edge of the wooden bench where the Professor lay. Wet as I was, I froze horribly but managed to shake down my blanket, wrapped it around me, leaned against the table and so I slept half the rest of that day trip.

It was short enough due to a damaged engine, which forced the Captain to seek port here in San Andreas Bay. At 1 am we came to the shelter of the small island in the mouth of Cono Inlet. I tore off my shoes, climbed into the bunk and slept there until 7 in the evening. Then I was fairly dry. When I then went to bed in earnest at 9 pm, I was on the verge of an unpleasant awakening when the Captain said we would continue early this morning. But nothing came of it. The damaged engine had not yet been repaired, and we have had plenty of time to watch the rain pour down. Our accommodation was like a pigsty. Water and oil were on the floor. Dirty backpacks, sailor bags, suitcases, rifles, rainwear, etc. did not make the space larger. It was damn filthy, and I'll be very happy the day I get ashore. Of course, I know that a dog's life awaits us there too, rain and wind, but it always gets better anyway.

20th December 1920, Kelly Inlet. Last night at six o'clock we came to the scene of our study work. We left Bahia San Andres and Estero Cono at six in the morning. It was blowing a healthy northwest with rain showers and fog banks, so I was prepared for the worst. But, did you see me, I managed the record! Of course, it rippled around well in the inside, but no sacrifice to Neptune was made.

I was the one who was happy and satisfied, of course. I was even so proud that I could help Pallin get some photographs of Cabo Raper and its coastal outlines. So, we sailed around Cabo Tres Montes and entered the stormy, infamous, Golfo de Penas. And it justified the name. It was a roller coaster. But I kept myself brave. And soon we could see our San Tadeo Glacier and Kelly Inlet. It was grandiose. There lay the glacier, mighty and large, shining white. We shall now join it. These are interesting things that await us.

No one has ever been here to investigate the huge masses of ice. Here is unknown ground. Here Swedish feet are trampling for the first time, perhaps human feet for the first time. I have always laughed a little at those who always strive to be the first in every new place, but now I understand them. There is an allure, an indescribable satisfaction in the thought: 'Here I am the first. Everything I see here, no one has seen. Everything I do has a certain value for science'. Let it not be that my ability is too small to fully utilize everything, but if you work conscientiously the work has its value in any case.

We came into the bay and steamed very slowly along the north shore to find anchorage. Then we were stuck in a clay bank. The maps, the ones that exist[15], are abysmal and in addition lots of sand and clay are deposited here in the bay from the glaciers. This means that the depth conditions are constantly changing. After two hours of work, we were afloat again. The weather was rainy and windy all day. It cleared a little in the evening, the moon came up and the occasional star flashed. For dinner, of course, champagne taken from the box that the Swedish minister in Buenos Aires had presented to the expedition. Then it became letter writing. When the boat leaves, it takes mail with it.

Today, we have been up early. At 6 am, we were woken up and at 7 we started to investigate the possibilities for a landing place. It was not encouraging. The fjord shores fell steeply into the water. Where the land is a little lower further into the fjord, the aforementioned sandbanks prevent all the protruding seaways. In addition, everything is overgrown with the terrible Patagonian primeval forest. It is not so dense, with an axe you can easily cut your way, but on the ground are fallen trees, branches and twigs in a layer. This can go up to 20 meters thick with more than meter thick layer of moss on top.

✧

Chapter 3

A DOG'S LIFE IN WEST PATAGONIA

by Nils Pallin

Taking shelter for a meal break

It was on 19th December that we landed in the gloomy
Kelly Fjord, which for the next few months would be our
home. We already had good knowledge about the difficult
climate that prevails on this remote part of the Earth. But
our own coming experiences would far exceed our worst
expectations. During this Patagonian summer, on a latitude
which almost corresponds to Vienna and Orleans, the average temperature was not up to 10°C and during the night it
was rarely above 5°C. About the temperature, however, there
was not much reason to complain, because Swedes generally have little respect for cold. But if other West Patagonian
travellers long before us rather bitterly complained about
the rain, we also had reason to do so. It rained almost every
day during the expedition period, and the amount of rain
falling for the month amounted to as much as during a full
year in Stockholm. For one unfamiliar with the situation this
raining is almost inconceivable. Either the raining is stream-
ing steadily and calm for days and days, or else it comes in
violent bursts of such intensity that it is as if large buck-
ets were emptied over the tent canvas. The air itself here
seems, as Darwin says, to be darker than elsewhere (Note 2
in Chapter 7).

Summer in the sense of beautiful weather did we have not
more than one week of, and that was around the turn of the
year. This means that the sun appeared at intervals, and for
a whole day, but only one, no rain fell on the place where
we were. And moreover, the weather reminded us of the raw-
est and chilliest November in Sweden. Snow fell a couple of
times. Every now and then you could hear thunder rumbling
in the distance. The wind at our coastal station was usually
weak and almost constantly blew from the sea towards land.

A couple of times the wind blew in the opposite direction, from the Cordilleras, with rising temperature and had the nature of a 'foehn'.

The cause for this cold and humid climate lies mainly in the country's position relative to the extremely cold Antarctic continent, that spouts violent cold storms towards the north over the humid sea. These storms later travel towards the north along the west coast, and along the West Antarctic mountains and up the South American Cordilleras. The air, as previously described, precipitates its humidity step by step. Above all, this takes place on the rocky coast of Western Patagonia, where the dripping climate is rainier than in any other temperate region. At some places it may be rainier than anywhere on the entire Earth (Note 3 in Chapter 7).

This rain has the effect of crippling all work. All observations are made more difficult, and mapping using conventional methods is almost impossible. Photography becomes a hazard and one must constantly lie out and watch for the few moments that are sufficiently illuminated. Already after a short time out in the open, the rain soaks through most kinds of hitherto known rain garments and penetrates into the other clothes, which are then almost impossible to get properly dry. Even in the tents, everything is eventually permeated with moisture and covered with mould. Packing that is carried in the open, soon doubles its weight and turns the scientist on tour into a veritable beast of burden. Life becomes soggy and places the greatest demands on endurance and equanimity. This depressing impact that the climate generates, in the long run makes you feel like being buried alive. When the weather on rare occasions clears up, it is as if some blessed spirit lifted the lid of the coffin.

The only good thing you could say about the climate is that it appears to be relatively healthy. Throughout our stay in the area of the Kelly Fjord not a single case of illness occurred, not even a cold. But the humidity stopped or hindered almost all transpiration, which instead took its outlet through the big main exit, and in particular could make itself felt at night. And you never got thirsty. During my stay in the Western Patagonia, I drank water only once and this was during strenuous mountaineering, the only one that was done in dry weather.

But beside the climate, there is another enormous difficulty which you have to tackle in Western Patagonia. It is the forest. In this humid, even dripping climate, a rampant vegetation which bears a significant name, the *rainforest*. This is also such a hell[01]. In considerable perkiness it closes the route wherever you go. Tree trunks standing closely together wrapped in thick moss balls, untearable lianas, thorny bushes and countless half rotten trees that lie fallen everywhere overgrown with moss and ferns makes you walk high above the real ground. They force you to work your way through with an axe in your hand, and swing yourself like a monkey through the holes you manage to produce. I don't know if any investigations have been made of the rotting of these immense masses of dead trees cluttering the ground, but it seemed to me that these processes in West Patagonia's all wet climate were progressing very slowly. As the country undoubtedly in these areas undergoes rapid level changes, you may believe you are witnessing the first stage of coal formation in the dead rain forests. It is a formation that may not be completed until after thousands of years (Note 4 in Chapter 7).

Rainforest

More rainforest

To these difficulties, others may be added. There are the barricading steeps, that the primeval forests covered mountains put in the way for every advancement. And then you only need to imagine this rainforest in the above described wetness to get a picture of the difficulties you have to subdue.

Rainforest on the shores of Kelly Inlet [AJ[02]]

But we also had another obstacle to contend at our coastal station in the Kelly Fjord. To this fjord, two large glaciers[03] had their outlet, in such a way that it was shown later to be of a most interesting kind.

Reconnoitring in Kelly Inlet with the South Glacier (Glacier Benito)
in the background and Isla Boscosa to the right

The sludge that the glacial rivers brought in their grey-ish-white water had already managed to settle in such great quantity out in the fjord. The fjord was almost filled by it up to the water surface and out to the banks outside the Boscosa Islands in the fjord's outer part, where our steamer grounded on its arrival. During high tide the fjord appeared to be filled with water, but at low tide the dirty grey, flat slam banks were sticking up in the water everywhere. Between these, the glaciers' delta rivers passed in winding canals. Once a month, at full moon, i.e. the spring flood tide, there was during a few short hours of the day high enough water to travel the fjord with a rowing boat. If the ebb tide should come, there was the danger to become steadfastly stuck. How this would reduce our movements in the different parts of this little known fjord, and be a hindrance to mapping, hunting and fishing etc. is easily seen. Only along the northern shore, from our station and out to sea, ran a narrow tidal gutter, which was reasonably navigable even during low tide. There appeared a strong stream of cloudy, but almost fresh glacier water, from which we derived our need for cooking. At other times, during flood, the water in the gutter was almost 'straight up and down' and was then unusable for drinking.

The complex delta at the east end of Kelly Inlet

This was the environment we took in possession just before Christmas, when we pitched our tents in one of the few places where it was possible to reach the ground and clear some minimal spots, smooth enough for the purpose. From the Chilean general staff, we had through mediation by the Swedish Colonel W. Ekdahl in Santiago, borrowed two excellent army tents, each for two officers, but holding four men. They were of the Mummery type[04] and provided with loose double roofs, which were fastened about two decimetres above the actual tent roof and were as excellent protection against tropical sunshine as against heavy rain. They turned out absolutely rainproof, but the water instead penetrated from below, where you only had to put your foot on the ground for the water to rise around the ankles. In addition to the two army tents, we brought three

Swedish four-piece trooper tents (Army model). Our three Chilotes were given one for housing, another was used as a store tent for fragile items, and the third was used during our expeditions from the coastal camp out into the surroundings. A couple of other small tents which we had brought along were used during excursions. In addition, the Chilotes erected from split tree trunks a leaning kitchen roof by the campfire, where they huddled up together when opportunity was given, and enjoyed the dryness and warmth.

The Chilotes' lean-to

Finally, a makeshift shed was built by intertwined tree branches to protect the main part of our baggage. By pulling a tarpaulin over its roof we were given a scanty protection against the rain. Immediately below the camp, we had our boat harbour, inside of a small cliff spit. There the water level gauge was erected, and a zero point was cut out in a vertical rock plaque. Together with the meteorological station with its thermometer cage and rain gauge, all this put together made the parts of our main camp or coastal camp, also called 'Camp 1', from which we then started our journeys.

Another tent at Camp 1 in amongst the moss-clad trees

In pouring rain, we here started our preparations for an advance to the San Tadeo Glacier, where we were to have our actual field of work. This outstanding glacier, which perhaps is the largest in South America, had never been trod by a human foot before us. Access to its areas of ice by normal routes is made impossible by vast and impassable swamps that the glacier's draining rivers have created in front of its tongue. It has been seen only from a distance, and its character is shown incorrectly on all current maps. It was with the knowledge of those difficulties that Nordenskjöld decided to land here in the Kelly Fjord, in a valley parallel to south of the San Tadeo Glacier's valley, and to cross the land which separates these two valleys, and to make a flank attack on the ice. This succeeded, too, but it took us a lot of time to solve this 'technical' task.

If you ask how everyday life manifests itself on an exploration expedition under the conditions described above, the answer cannot be more than one. Efforts paid off with success always feeds satisfaction, although discomfort and strenuous jobs are associated therewith. A well-planned operation, which is methodically led and carried out and therefore ultimately has the possibility to snatch some new secrets from nature, has in this scientific purpose its main fascination. It is this strange delight, face to face with the unsolved riddles of nature, that creates the explorer. In it he has a source of constant renewal. If you feel gloomy in your mind, when the eternal rain is shedding its flood of tears over tent prisons, you have to make your life spirits take a new hold and to be satisfied with the resources at hand.

You crave very little to be satisfied. How many times did I not sit during idle moments by the Kelly Fjord or in other camps and smoke my dear pipe under the taut canvas shrunk by rain. I enjoyed the blue smoke, which embodies the most beautiful thoughts, without having to make the effort of thinking them. This psychology of the pipe comes to its fullest right under such conditions. Its major significance is perhaps not fully understood until you find yourself in this kind of surroundings, to such a degree depressing that a simple pipeful of tobacco comes as a last resort for body and soul. It is strange that you can remember such an insignificant thing. Smoking was for us the stimulant of the highest value, that sweetened many a damp moment. There is some doubt if civilized man can endure the worst sides of life close to nature, without uplifting their normal mood with such mildly toxic means as tobacco. In all cases, it is certain that the pipe, the tent and the campfire are inseparable concepts. For us at our station in Kelly Fjord as well as in our various camps in the neighbourhood this little tool was as essential as a great source of recreation.

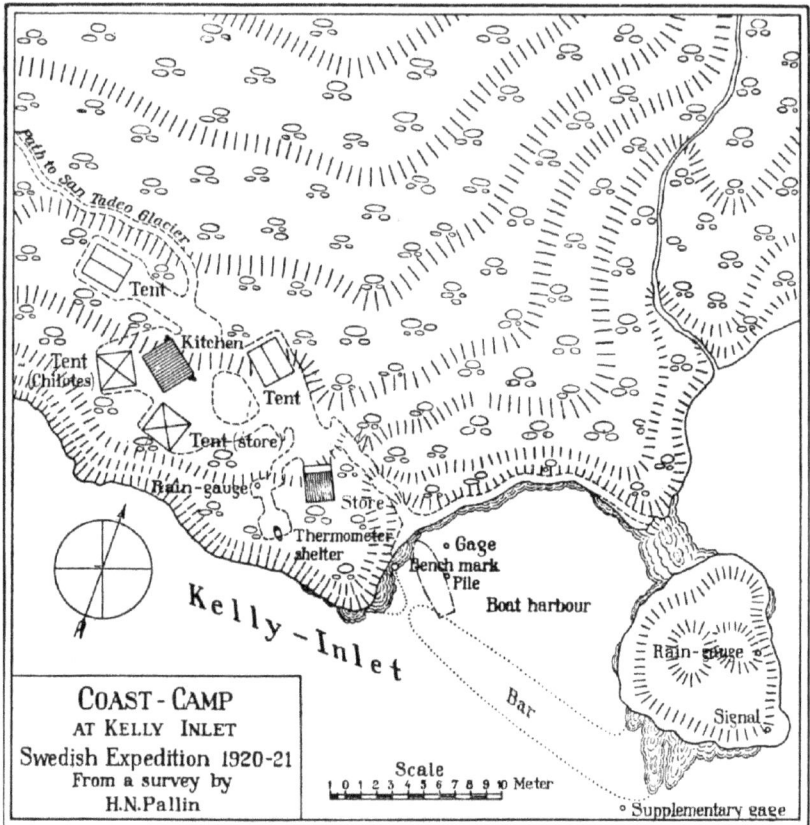

Coast Camp (Camp 1) in the West Patagonian rainforest [AJ]

In other words, if we had this quite significant means with us to make life easier, it would then be unjust not to confess, that also nature itself at times contributed to our encouragement. The Kelly Fjord had its beauty, even when it lay wrapped in its grey mist. From our station we could not see the fjord's outlet, only the low land of the inside[05]. But above this towered in the distance the rocky island of San Javier situated on the outside [of Kelly Fjord], rarely glimpsed through the rains, but nice to behold, since its appearance generally prophesied better weather. The station was in a small bay on the north shore, a few hundred metres from a high waterfall. In the other direction, it was close to the fjord's inner arms and the Kelly Glacier[06] situated in a straight line. The magnificent rock dome Pylorus rose on the southern shore before our eyes. It was symmetrical as a pudding mould, lying in the angle of a valley going south, and towards another mighty glacier in the distance which threw its mucus-filled water masses out into the fjord all the way to our beach. From this nearby mountain that ended our view to the east, ranged the distant silhouette of bold mountain peaks out to the fjord inlet. Among those were the Master, the Epigon, the Gemini and the Man's Top, and left a beautiful sample of the orographic rhythm of the Patagonian coastal Cordilleras. When these mountains stood dry from the mists, dark as mellow blueberries with white flames of fresh snow over the staggering cliffs, our eyes were invited to a delicious meal.

View to the south from the deck of Yañez *in Kelly Inlet.*
In the distance is the distinctive Monte Cathedral

However, it is understandable that it is difficult to comprehend how civilized people can want to undergo an exploration expedition to these sad regions. In fact, the distressing climate also explains why the otherwise well-located Western Patagonia is one of the most unknown areas on earth. But sometimes, however, the sun could show itself even above this the gloomiest of coasts, and a couple of times we had an almost cloudless sky. I think that the wondering person would only need to experience one of these sunshine days to falter in his perception and understand that if the darkness is dark, light is also so much brighter. A more cheering feeling and a greater relief, even for the most insensitive mind, you could not imagine. It is worth something, too, that from an eternally wet and hateful darkness for a moment step out in a lovingly warm sunshine, where forest and waters, life and flowers make sense. Because then you feel as if you discovered that nature has a purpose, and that you yourself have a nobler self in the depths of your heart.

View of Kelly Glacier which the expedition visited in the 2nd part of the expedition[06]

One of the Kelly fjord's most beautiful hours, I went with two of our Chilotes in a rowing boat into the fjord's inner part, where none of us had yet reached. It was a spring flood and late in the evening and the fjord lay in a lively and reflective evening light. After we had rounded the port headland, whose shallow water so far blocked our way, the view suddenly opened up towards the far east, the glacier resting in the fjord's inner valley. Above this the main Cordilleras towered, with their snowy mountains, crystal clear over the glacier's oblique contour with a pair of staggering mountain giants, that stormed heaven and bided their downfall in stiff frozen greatness. The dark, primeval forest-covered beaches, the dead forest covered inland to the foot of the glacier, and Pylorus in the water next to us with vertically steeping slopes created a dark and absorbing frame around the blushing Andes. Everything together formed a painting of such a peculiar mood, that the heart widened before these rivers of defiant beauty. Also, this was something new, as perhaps never before seen by a man. A world that had lived for itself, a dream of beauty that no one has thought and no one seen, and that now for the first time had been born into a reality in the human eye. In such moments, strong emotions stream over the viewer; he experiences the delight to be the first, and it fills his heart and mind with a clean crushing strength. Discoverer's joy is greater than anything else. Only the allure to take a beloved creature in your arms can be compared with the triumph to take a new, untouched world in possession.

Yes, the discoverer's joy is the greatest, both in the world of the body and that of the spiritual world. The earth loses some of its charm every time a white spot is blackened by the researcher of nature. Less and less remains left to do, and in this for man most natural of all activity fields there is less width in the world but more and more nook. Soon, only a faint scent of wonder world remains from the memory of the still not-so-distant days, when the earth appeared to be an inexhaustible field for the discoverer, the conqueror and the intruder. Yet there are still a few unknown geographic areas, and towards those the last discoverers are pulling forward in determined crowds.

And then? Yes, then! It's the same state of things everywhere. Who bothers about tomorrow! On our return trip to the west, the Kelly Fjord lay in a dreamy wedding mood with shiny water between the twinkling evening gusts. On the horizon at the fjord's mouth on the way of the light, the cream-coloured San Javier rose, shining like fresh violets in sunshine. When we returned into our little harbour, our twilight way was illuminated by Venus with a splendour of beams, that seemed almost earthly in its enchanted brightness. These clear evening moments we could sometimes get, when the south hemisphere's rich star splendour in its quiet grandeur spread out over our camp, and the Southern Cross with its two companions in Centaur hovered like holes in the sky over the dying campfire. We would linger by the embers and load our cooled pipes again and rejoice in life, with childish unconcern for tomorrow.

View of Kelly Inlet from above Camp 1 with San Javier Island in the distance and Isla Boscosa on the left[07]

But these quick moments were unfortunately too rare. They were like jewels in a crown of grey stone. Rain was our daily bread from morning to evening and from evening to morning. As soon as the work did not take care of the thoughts, they also preferably went to other areas than Patagonia, to other wildernesses than the Kelly Fjord or to cultural centres, that are the contradictions of wilderness. Above all, you wanted to change to winter from this weeping autumn, to the snow and cold from this dripping coolness. How often was not brought to mind the Swedish wilderness, for our own divine Lapland, this lovely country with its sun and its shimmering snow. What glorious days it gives to work and rest, and how does it not awaken love for nature in the hearts of men. By Kelly Fjord you did not get a heightened sense of love for nature. Maybe you were instead getting feelings quite the contrary in front of this nature, so ungenerous to man that it was making an otherwise rich and fertile land virtually uninhabitable for these unquestioned rulers of nature. Rather than to live in such a wet land, you would be willing to go to the pole with its cruel cold. Against the moisture, every method is powerless in the long run. Against the cold you can still arm yourself. Cold is fair and cruel, wet is insidious and embarrassing.

Extracts From Allan Bäckman's Letters

Wednesday, December 22, 1920 - The camp at Kelly Inlet. This is thus the second day in our main camp. We left *Yañez* at six o'clock yesterday morning during a nice drizzle, which made everything wet and damp. When we arrived at the camp, we immediately began work to put it in order. The Chilotes built a shed for the luggage; Rosen and I set up two small tents, helped the Professor to open boxes and review their contents. The ones that were too wet were put into an empty tent; the others were placed under a tarpaulin.

Then it was time to cook. The sack with 'frijoles', beans similar to our Swedish brown, but white, arrived, fire was already settled, water in a pot and so it began. I stood for that goal, picked out a 'corned beef' jar[08], emptied the contents of the pot as well and boiled the most delicious middle ground between soup and, well, what should you call it? Of course, it was burned, but the praise was in any case overwhelming. The meal ended with coffee, something thin, but wonderfully warming, then the pipe came out, general satisfaction. After this lunch, which was served at 12 o'clock, I prepared for the night, gathered branches of *Nothofagus*[09] as bedding, laid a layer of ferns on top and so the sleeping bag. It was really successful. I slept so warm and comfortable last night. Then the thermometer cage must be 'carpented' together and set up. It also became my job. I got hold of an empty box, made a long side for the door, nailed it with the bottom up between two bars, tightened steel wire for the thermometers. It sounds simple and as if it was done in a few minutes, but it got almost dark before I stopped. Then it was time to cook again, potatoes, fried pork and coffee. I boiled the potatoes - excellent! So, I withdrew to the tent, undressed, said goodnight, and fell asleep.

Allan in front of Nils and Allan's tent at Camp 1

When I have made the dinner observations at 2 pm, I will dry my shoes and socks. Do you know how it feels to go splash wet on your feet all day long? In any case, it's not terribly nice. And here all efforts to stay dry fail. The moss is so wet that a lake forms around the foot as soon as you put it down. And then nothing helps! But you get used to it soon enough. Fortunately, there is no cold here. According to the minimum thermometer, we had only +7°C last night as the coldest. During the day it is now about +10°C. But when the rain stops and the south wind comes then it may be a little gloomier. (In the northern hemisphere the south wind is usually warm. Here in the south it is of course usually cold.) The same if we get up on the ice. But we do not yet know how the latter will succeed. If it continues to rain, it may be impossible. But I am healthy and well despite the wetness. Admittedly, my nose runs a bit, but you must not stick to that. More serious seems to me a wound, which I received on the left hand yesterday. It has swelled slightly last night despite iodine brushing last night. It would be a little uncomfortable to get blood poisoning like this out in the wilderness.

Thursday, December 23, 1920. This rain is the most stubborn I've ever been through. It prevented us yesterday from all the work with the exception of a few small jobs in the camp. Here we go and slap in the wet moss, our noses run like small streams and the mood is below zero. Then you just wait for food. Yesterday's dinner was charming, goulash with rice, fruit soup and for coffee a pipe. Of course, I ate the most of us all, but at least now I regret (at 11 am) that I did not eat more. But the prunes in the fruit soup made an impact; I have to get up at half past six this morning. By the way, it was probably good, because then I had the opportunity to get the observations for at 7 am. I have since continued them every hour. In my free time, I have also fabricated a rain gauge from an empty can. Unfortunately, I did not get hold of any larger 'vessel', and in these rainy conditions I have to empty it every four hours.

Allan with his rain gauge

✧

Chapter 4

TO THE ETERNAL ICE

by Nils Pallin

The upper region of the San Tadeo Glacier with Mount San Valentin in the distance

The main goal for our expedition was the San Tadeo Glacier and its source areas within the so-called 'Patagonian Inland Ice'. This last-mentioned expression is admittedly somewhat misleading, in that with 'inland ice' in the strict sense refers to a continental ice, covering the land to such a height and thickness that the contours of the underlying ground disappear. The highest mountains stick up as peaked islands ('nunataks') from the smooth ice mass. Previously, the idea was that the Patagonian 'inland ice' was of this type. Had any question about this still remained, it was now completely eliminated by our observations. Those vast ice masses are essentially heavily glaciated mountain chains from which glaciers descend into enormous ice fields. New glaciers descend from basins of ice gathered on both sides of the main Cordilleras, partly to the west to the sea or its vicinity, and partly to the melting areas of the ice in the east.

Like a wall, the ridge of the Cordilleras passes through the ice in the longitudinal direction from north to south. This wall of ice is only broken in one point by the valley towards which the deepest sea bay of the earth, the Baker fjord, penetrates and divides the ice into a northern and a southern main area. This fjord has a depth of xxxx metres at its mouth[01] and thus surpasses the Sognefjord in Norway, whose largest depth amounts to 'only' 1244 metres. Into the inner part of the Baker fjord debouch the discharges of the great lakes Lago Buenos Aires[02], Lago Puerryedon and Lago San Martin, located east of the Cordilleras.

It was towards the larger of those two Patagonian ice fields we pushed forward[03]. The largest of the glaciers starting from this northern ice field is probably the San Tadeo Glacier, whose physical features it was our job to investigate closer. That this would be of special interest to us Swedes is evident, not least for the expedition leader, Nordenskjöld. He was the first person who, although in the south area and from the southeast, tried to penetrate into these South America's whitest spots - in double meaning - and there made the first and basic investigations a quarter of a century before, or more particularly in 1896 (Note 5 in Chapter 7).

At our campsite in the Kelly Fjord, we were separated from the Tadeo Glacier by the mountainous land between the fjord, and the glacier's north-facing valley. Although the distance as the crow flies could be estimated at a maximum of 10 km, it took us twelve days from the day we started to make a route through the primeval forest and until the day when Nordenskjöld and I stood for the first time on the San Tadeo Glacier. No human foot had trodden on that glacier's flood of ice before. Yet before that, we had had to spend five days reconnoitring the area, as good as was possible in the constantly flowing rain.

Anyone could understand that there had been great difficulties standing in our way to cause such delay. Above all it was the rain that detained us. But to a significant extent our slow advance was due to the forest, which I depicted in the previous chapter, and this combined with the steep mountain walls forced us to build real scaling ladders up against the hills in some places.

Our first reconnaissance was done on Christmas Eve, when Nordenskjöld, Bäckman and I, and a couple of the Chilotes, rowed down the fjord to the waterfall[04] on the north shore. We climbed up along this to investigate if there was a lake in the valley visible from the fjord on the inside of the waterfall as had been predicted by the German explorer Doctor Hans Steffen, to find out if this supposed lake really existed, and otherwise also to try to get a general view of the inland, and of the possibilities for advancing towards the ice. After having climbed a fairly forest-free mountain slope, we approached the upper part of the waterfall - about 40 metres high and falling down over several ledges - and then we entered the forest, to get a view of the valley.

The vegetation here gave us a true educational lesson. Although both Chilotes carried large axes and kept those in constant activity, and although we wriggled like eels between the branches, we did not get further into the valley than about 600 metres in three hours. It was then almost impossible for the men to cut any further through the extremely cluttered forest. Instead, we tried to climb right up the side

Setting off on Christmas Eve for the waterfall
(subsequently known as Darwin's Falls)

of the valley, but bumped our heads in a rock face and had
to turn back. From a stone fall point in the slope, we then
got a full view of the valley. It was large, wooded and of a
mild character, but it was closed to the north by a very steep
mountain wall with a notched ridge, over which the passage
was closed. No lake was seen at the bottom of the valley, and
our task for the day was thus solved; the valley was called
Waterfall Valley by us.

After having made these observations, we returned to the
camp, where we made our Christmas Eve dinner to the best
of our ability. Thanks to two large wooden boxes, which I had
brought to Rosen from Sweden and that only now were opened
to show their really delicious content, Christmas was given a
festive touch. Our Christmas dinner consisted of butter, bread,
cheese and sardines as well as O.P. Andersson's aquavit, boiled
Christmas ham with white beans and plum pudding with

Trees around Kelly Inlet

burning sauce, as well as champagne Pommery Extra Sec and 'Coffee with Avec'. In the series of toasts, the success of the expedition was the subject of a lively but because of the rain somewhat elusive discussion.

Several rain showers had fallen during the passing of the day, but otherwise the evening of Christmas Eve was sunny and blue, like a Midsummer's Eve ought to be. However, Christmas holiday did not mean rest and peace for us. Our time was short, our mission had really no limits and the obstacles in our way were countless. Every auspicious moment must therefore be used. They were not many and you were forced to use them with the greatest vigilance.

A view of Kelly Inlet at the start of the route to the Big Top

Another view looking eastwards towards the Kelly Glacier (Glacier Andrée)

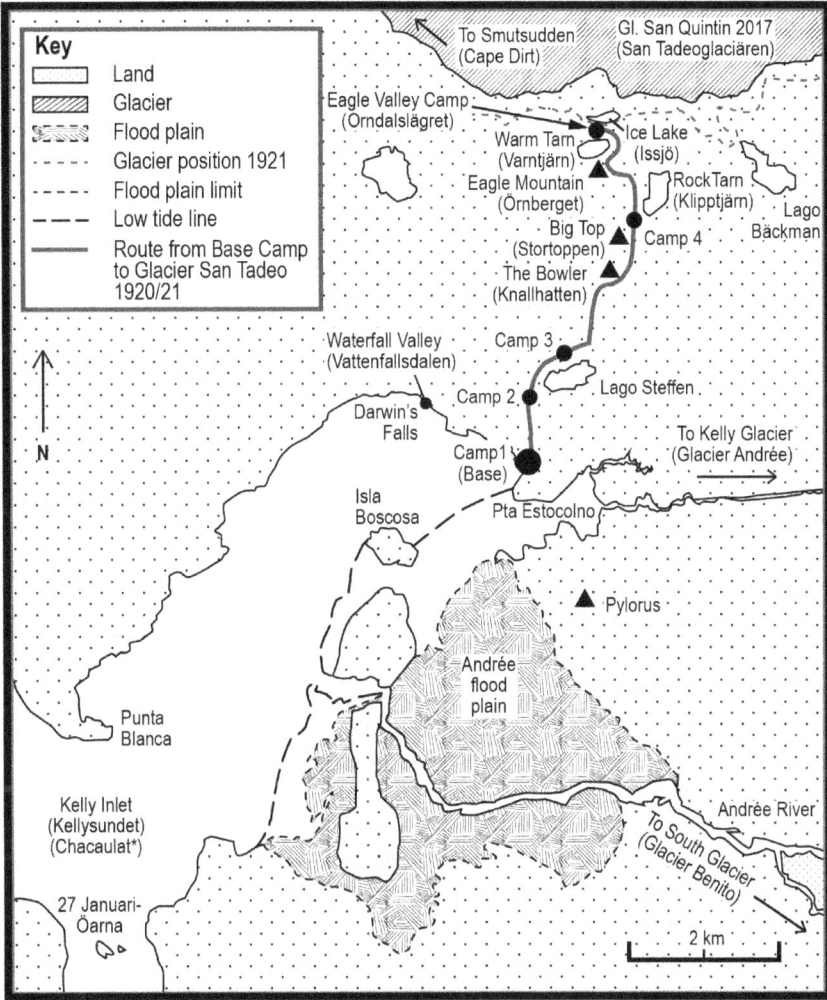

The route from Camp 1 (Base Station) to the San Tadeo Glacier

We had by our first excursion made clear to ourselves what path we should use to try to advance to the ice. Apparently, it was heading straight from our seaside camp, and up the mountain side by the beach where we had pitched our tents, and into a pass located in the rock-face east of Waterfall Valley. From this more sparsely overgrown mountain crest we had to reconnoitre further, and towards the north. The work with this path started as soon as the rain allowed it, and after a few days the cutting was done, and Camp 2 could be moved forward up to and inside of the pass. This path, which we had to climb innumerable times, was probably a misery beyond comparison. It was anyway a real royal route through this forest, which was otherwise as dripping and impenetrable as a dripping wet bale of cotton.

View looking westwards along the north side of Kelly Inlet

From the pass now reached, one's gaze passed over along, with the Kelly Fjord parallel valley, which in the north was bounded by the same mountain wall as the Waterfall Valley. In the northeast, it was rising into a couple of high mountains, among which was the one that had drawn our attention already on the *Yañez*, and that due to its form had been provisionally named 'the Bowler'. It was the fjord's most characteristic peak from the sea. Just below this mountain our continued path obviously had to be laid out, and we had here in front of us our next task. In the bottom of the parallel valley there was a small lake, its outlet flowing into the Waterfall Valley in the west. As it anyway in a sense was an equivalent of Steffen's supposed lake, it was by Nordenskjöld named 'Lago Steffen'. Our camp was placed in an idyllic location above the lake, where the soporific fairy noise of the brook was heard up to our tent during evenings without rain.

Kelly Inlet with Lago Steffen in the foreground

It was Nordenskjöld and I, that still in the last hour of the year were the first to climb the top of the Bowler and who caught the final overview of the land. New Year's Eve in 1920 when we made this ascent was a beautiful day. Only a small splash of rain fell in the morning, but otherwise the weather was exceptionally playful and blue. It was truly valuable luck, as we were to get far wider views than ever before, or later. Below the camp, the mirror clear Lago Steffen lay like a water filled crater between the high beach walls. Against its sky blue surface, the cypresses' crowns were drawing their refined Japanese silhouettes.

On one of the winding paths cleared through the forest by the Chilotes, we went down to the surface of the lake, passed its outlet and continued walking towards the north. We walked through thinning groves and small greenish-yellow mires, until we reached the south side of the mountain. This was grass covered to a height of about 600 metres and consisted beyond that of bare cliffs. Approximately at the same height patches of snow started to occur, on this mountain however considerably sparser than on the other peaks, situated higher up and further inland. As we rapidly passed the tree line, the ascent did not raise any difficulties. At two o'clock in the afternoon we were at the top, where we erected a cairn.

When you climb a mountain peak, you usually experience the pleasure of having overcome an obstacle and reached a goal. I have elsewhere tried to describe the feelings you experience in this. They exceed maybe all other pleasures. It is the joy of living itself, flowing through your blood. It is the feeling of triumph before a defeated obstacle. Secondly you are filled with a rare joy over the view which you possess here. And the third thing is that you make observations.

Summit of Cerro Pan, also known as The Bowler (Knallhatten) [AJ][05]

Up here, it was above all the third step that dominated. The view we had from the Bowler's top included vast, unknown areas. This was especially true of what we saw in a north-westerly direction, at the secretive Taitao Peninsula and the incredibly swampy and lagoon-rich Ofqui Isthmus, where the whole landscape looked like muck. A rather great unknown lake on the Ofqui Peninsula appeared to unburden a mighty flow into the Rio San Tadeo[06]. But in particular we were interested in what we might observe in the quadrant between the northeast and the southeast, where the 'inland ice' spread its dazzling white, wildly upset glacier cover over the Cordilleras. As it was seen that another peak, a few hundred metres further north, was about thirty metres higher, we climbed over on to this 'Big Top'. From this we completed our picture, especially of the Tadeo Glacier that at last lay beneath our feet, like a 10-km-wide descending torrent of ice.

Surveying from the 'Big Top' using a measuring or 'plane' table[07]

Here is not the place to list our richly rewarding observations at the time. It might be enough to point to the snowy mountains on the border between Chile and Argentina, without a black spot implying the rock foundation beneath. Straight to the northeast, at a distance of 70 km, was the cathedral-shaped peak of the highest mountain in Patagonia, Cerro San Valentin, seen and measured from the north and found to be about 4,000 metres high[08]. From this a totally straight and abysmally steep slope stretched southwards, a wildly fluttering mountain ridge on which the peaks were sticking up like fish fins against the sky, strangely clear for a short moment, and completely closing the view towards Lago Buenos Aires[02], the great mountain lake below the mountain ridge. We later had the possibility to study slightly further south, from the interior of the Kelly Fjord, the same watershed. This range of mountains, seen straight eastwards from the fjord descended into lower and less violent terrain, probably there forming the only pass of the northern ice areas, through which a crossing of the Cordilleras can be done in these parts[09].

Below and between this otherwise seemingly insurmountable wall, completely covered by ice and hoarfrost, and the lower coastal mountains lay the immense ice fields. These supply all glaciers descending towards the sea and its bays, from Golfo de Elefantes in the north all the way to the Baker Fjord in the south. It is this ice field that I have proposed should be named after Nordenskjöld, through whose expedition its proper character has been fully elucidated[10]. Immediately beneath our feet in a southerly direction the inland area of the Kelly Fjord was finally revealed to our eyes with its low land, covered by mirelands and old river branches, against which the tongue of the Kelly Glacier had stopped its ragged masses. We here made the observation that this glacier was not independent but did act as a delta branch from the upper part of the Tadeo Glacier. It did not have its outlet in the bay of the Kelly Fjord where it apparently ended, but through a valley located south of this, which was separated from the Kelly Fjord by a low ridge, on whose north terrace an ink-coloured lake showed its solitary and gloomy countenance.

The shattered but snowless Jesuit Mountains ended our view towards the south. The view was continued by the Golfo de Penas and the ocean, whose surf lay as a white strip along the shallow beach below the messy foreland of the San Tadeo Glacier. The high Javier Island, situated outside the fjord in the south-west, with its forests and sunny spots, its rounded profile and its steep rocks, looked like a South America in miniature. Far out to sea in an opal-coloured sun smoke, we sensed rather than saw the remotely situated Cabo Tres Montes, where our glances tumbled away to swim in the blue infinity of the horizons.

From the 'Big Top' straight to the north below our feet, we saw a little, deep but smiling cirque valley. In the north, it was blocked by the Tadeo Glacier, against whose cheese-like laminas of ice a small lake, dammed in by the glacier, rippled its mirror surface. Above this lake, on whose grey water blocks of ice were floating around, and separated from the lake by a lateral moraine looking like a dam gate, was a warm tarn with brown water. This received numerous streams from the water-collecting valley sides all around. Both lakes were traversed by an outlet brook, coming from a high up on a ledge situated lake or tarn in our neighbourhood. On the moraine between the two lower lakes, we had apparently the right place for our ice camp.

Looking towards South Glacier (Glacier Benito) on left and Pylorus on right

*Looking south-east to the South Glacier
(Glacier Benito)*

*Early glimpse of Kelly Glacier flowing from the left as the
'Bowler' is ascended*

More of Kelly Glacier is revealed[11]

Looking east – Kelly Glacier with, to the right, Glacier Rabot[12]

Looking north-east – Kelly Glacier with left to right glaciers Strindberg[13], Frænkel and Rabot

Looking towards Mount San Valentin in the far distance

Looking towards the north side of the San Tadeo Glacier

It was with satisfaction that we returned back to our in-between camp after having made all these observations. From 1920, the riddle of the west side of the Patagonian inland ice is finally solved. This glacier ice was of a new type, which represented a strong glaciation of an alpine character. It was so strongly developed, that in its upper parts it was close to the Svalbard and the Franz Joseph Land type. In its lower parts, thanks to the terrain form of the land, it strongly recalled the basin-like Alaskan kind.

We now returned to the coast camp to prepare our transfer to the Tadeo Glacier. For this operation which on the now cleared route took four days, we had to build two more in-between camps, No. 3 by the shore of Lago Steffen and No. 4 by the above-mentioned cliff tarn. During this transfer, the weather was unusually good to be in Patagonia, and we were able to take advantage of long rain pauses during the days. At 'Rock Tarn' camp, we experienced real idylls. We had raised our tent by a small brook about a hundred metres above the Rock Tarn, which in the east was surrounded by high and vertical rock walls and in the west by a rock dam, through which the lake had cut its way down towards the depths of the cirque valley.

San Tadeo Glacier with Rock Tarn in foreground and an emerging nunatak on the northside of the glacier[14] [AJ]

It was Twelfth Night when we arrived there, and the feast was celebrated with extra coffee in the evening, after the Chilotes had returned to camp 3 to fetch new burdens. Thereafter, we took ourselves a pipe of tobacco and chatted. We ate walnuts that Nordenskjöld with a true understanding of the meaning of such details, pulled out from his inexhaustible supply of pleasant surprises. When we turned off the light at night, I lay awake a long time and listened to the murmur of the brook in the rainless night, and the sounds that were heard from nature. Perhaps it was a fox who struck down the plates by the fire, if it was not one of those imperceptible *temblores*, haunting but avoiding being perceived? But there was also someone who was there sniffing out our food supply. Through a tent slit, I saw a gap in the clouds. Through this shone Sirius like a friendly spirit, an old dear and faithful friend with messages from other persons, whose uncertain roads were simultaneously illuminated by its light across half the planet.

From this camp Nordenskjöld and I did the reconnaissance, during which after a breakneck descent into the earlier mentioned cirque valley, we, as the first human beings, trod the Tadeo Glacier's ice, and the western flank of the North Patagonian ice. Everywhere, the obstacles to our progress were big. Where the way at a distance looked easy and unhindered by forests and steep slopes, even the smallest forest grove made for us an incredible jam, while gaps and precipices often forced us to take long detours. When we finally hit our ice axes in the glacier's grey ice, the expedition's first goal was achieved, as far as we finally stood at our most important field of work. It was now time to set up a suitable operating base and start our investigations.

For transport to the ice over the ridge at 700 metres height, we brought with us all our Chilotes. The entire expedition, except Rosen, whose zoological interest retained him at the main station, pulled away to the Tadeo Glacier. From here, the Chilotes were sent back so as not to erode the scarce food supply carried up. After a week they would return with reinforcement of our proviant. Only Nordenskjöld, Bäckman and I stayed by the ice.

We arrived at the selected camp site on the moraine between the lakes on January 8, 1921, eighteen days after our landing in the Kelly Fjord. The weather was sunny and clear that day and the march down the mountain slope became sweaty and heavy. Upon our arrival at the moraine, a goose family swam on Warm Tarn, a family idyll rapidly dispelled by the men who immediately started to hunt for the goslings. God be praised, however, without luck! Wherever mankind occurs in nature, they come like intruders. As such, we arrived at this pristine valley to stay there for the shortest time. A couple of eagle-like birds, hovering over this green bowl, gave the name Eagle Valley.

The last leg of the journey to Eagle Camp nearing the edge of Warm Tarn

Extracts from Allan Bäckman's Letters

Christmas Eve, 1920. Well, I got up at 7 o'clock and found the weather glorious. The sun was high in the sky, the fjord was shiny and beautiful, surrounded by high mountains and white-clad mountain peaks. But there was no Christmas mood! In the kitchen, the coffee water boiled, in honour of the day we also got oatmeal, and so the work began.

We are trapped here. To the north of us rises a huge mountain slope, steep and transverse, and covered with genuine Patagonian primeval forest. To the east, south and west we have the fjord, but it is inwards so shallow that we cannot even navigate it with our rowing boat. It is now important to find a way either over the mountain to the north or also to the east between the sandbanks of the fjord. Today we have made the first attempt. We took the boat and tried to bypass a headland, which obscures the view to the east. In vain! Everywhere we went aground and for the time being abandoned the experiments. So, we headed down to a small ice-eroded valley (hanging valley), from which a waterfall rushed down into the fjord. The valley went in a northerly direction. We hoped that the route would go over the mountain and down to the glacier. It became difficult and wet.

The waterfall (known as Darwin's Falls) near Camp 1[04]

This forest is significantly worse than the Peruvian primeval forest. There you get a real route, if you just chop away the thickets, bushes and trees that block the progress. But it's different here. If you clear branches and thickets here, you will reveal thousands of fallen half-rotten trees, overgrown with meter-thick moss. You have to balance on these tree trunks. Your feet sink deep into the soaked moss and suddenly you step through and sink to the waist or further down in a moss-covered hole. Progress is slow. We spent about four hours going about 500 meters. Then we gave up the experiment. We had also seen enough to state that path was probably possible, but extremely difficult. The valley was a typical glacier valley. It ended upwards after a rather sharp bend to NW in a 'cirque'; at the bend an eastern hanging valley ended.

But it had been a long time since the ice had slid there, for the water erosion had already cut steep gorges at the eastern end of the valley. When we found this and that the rock consisted of a porphyry granite, we returned to the boat and after a few minutes of rowing we were in the camp. There, the preparation of Christmas Eve dinner took place, hard bread with butter and two sardines, frijoles and cooked ham and plum pudding. Beverages and champagne were served for the drinks. The plum pudding was part of Rosen's Christmas box, which by the way turned out to be unusually rich in content. With coffee at 8 pm were served biscuits, chocolate and walnuts from the Christmas box and the 'Christmas newspapers' (comprising newspapers, magazines, sports magazines, etc., for the month of September) were provided.

So, I invited Prof for cigars (only I am such a hardened smoker that I enjoy cigars). We had had enough alcohol at dinner.

Christmas Day, 1920. It is holiday peace today in the camp. I was up at 8 o'clock, took the observations and a cup of coffee. So, I sat down to read 'Christmas magazines', until I heard an unusual concern in the kitchen corner. It was the Professor's team baking pancakes. 'Herre mein Gott' he swore to himself! The batter was as thin as clean water, the cooker was only warm, he had no idea about the lard. It was all impossible. I took the thing in my hands, stirred the batter thick enough, heated the pan properly, rubbed it well with lard and started. The result was brilliant. At 10 in the morning, we stood around the pancake dish and ate until the chewing muscles ached. Then a period of lethargy was followed by a lunch of lentils (not Danish but small Chilean peas) with potatoes and a can of 'goulash'. I grabbed the diary, and here I write.

Now I will take the observations at two o'clock, then I will boil with the hypsometer to determine the barometer corrections, then a new minimum thermometer will be set up. The tea should be ready at 4, which I also have to manage, as I am the kitchen manager for today and tomorrow. The weather has been changeable today, sometimes sunshine and sometimes rain. Since it is somewhat so clear, the temperature has dropped a few degrees and it probably feels so cold. Worst on the feet, because the shoes cannot be allowed to dry. I have to put them on soaking wet every morning and then it does not help much to have dry socks. In a few moments, your feet are completely soaked and chilled. Now it does not do much because now I'm used to it. But it was devilish, so unpleasant at first.

Sunday, 26th December 1920. My job with the instruments and the kitchen occupied me fully. I made a clever aneroid comparison yesterday, and from now on I will do one every week to be able to trust the barometer data[15]. A new minimum thermometer was set up as the old one indicated too high (approx. 0.7°). According to what the morning observations today, the new one also seems to be a little wrong (0.1°) but now we have no other option. When the instruments were ready, the kitchen management started. Dinner was to be cooked. The menu was somewhat peculiar, rice porridge and fruit soup.

But I managed the cooking well. I boiled the rice groats in (diluted) condensed milk and managed to garnish the fruit soup with potato flour. Needless to say, my cuisine aroused general admiration. Then came the coffee. Rosen offered us biscuits and the Prof some punch. A cigar and a few pipes of smoke put the crown on top of the work. I could not sleep really well. Because out here in the wilderness I have a voracious appetite. Consequently I like to overload the centre of life a bit. In addition, the climate here is so humid that evaporation from the body is reduced to a minimum and instead you have to pee so much more. Every night you have to get up at least once. Last night, the alcohol also contributed and forced me out into the pouring rain and darkness twice. The result of everything was an oversleep.

Next day. Now I have retired to my tent and will start with the repair of our minimum thermometers. Namely, I am the most practical of the expedition members (according to my own opinion) and therefore occupy the instrument maker's important place. 'Mal tiempo' (Spanish - bad weather)! What devilish weather! What if we had sunshine and beautiful! Then we could have done something. Now we sit in the tents and stare aimlessly into the rain mist, dreaming of ice and snow, and long hikes on unknown glaciers!

But the rain flows incessantly. The large heavy drops form wavy rings in bodies of water, slamming on the roof like gunfire in the Battle of Marne[16]. And the mood! And the worst thing is that you eventually lose hope of improvement. And I who will map the area! Map an area when you are so trapped that you cannot move ten meters!! It's light blue! I can stand for hours and look at the landscape to discover a single suitable point, as a starting point for my work. Impossible! And I have it clear to me, if I manage in this situation, then I have done a great work, fully comparable to Hercules!

Wednesday, 29th December 1920. I woke up, as I said, to sunshine, blue sky and the mirror-bright fjord. The mountains stand blue and solemn around us; the last precipitation has 'powdered' their peaks[17]. There is Sunday peace all over. I have used the sunshine to take some photos, some typical pictures of the forest. Now lunch will be served soon. Lunch is 'wet', delicious! Preserved haddock, macaroni. As I predicted, we did not get to keep the beautiful weather for long. There are already small showers of rain. I just made a deplorable discovery. My high American boots have soles of cardboard! That was, of course, why they were so cheap. Well, I can wear the cardboard for as long as possible. By the way, I have my others. They were half-soled splendidly after the Peru tour and will probably last the remaining month. If they did not do that, then I might as well run barefoot. The Chilotes do!

There is no defect in my other equipment. I have everything I need in my wardrobe. The only thing I miss is some instruments. But I thought the Professor would be abundantly provided in that case, but it was a miscalculation. Consequently, I am now the expedition's instrument maker, etc. I got the Prof to buy some instruments in Valparaiso, but as a result of our usual misfortune, the very sack where they were stowed was stolen on board the steamer 'Chiloé', which carried our large luggage to Puerto Montt. Thanks to the theft, I have a heavier load, as I now have to wander around with the theodolite,

where I instead would have used the clinometer[18], which can
be conveniently tucked in the vest pocket.

Dinner today: biscuits with cheese and a schnapps; rice and
a canned Frankfurter sausage, fruit soup + Champagne with C;
coffee. The impending break with the late motivated gala dinner. I will now crawl to bed to sleep out for tomorrow's efforts.

Thursday, 30th December 1920. Now a moment of rest has
come after a few hard hours. The day started with a little drizzle, but not worse than that so we decided to start the climb to
camp by the lake (Lago Steffen). But the preparations dragged
on, and we had time for morning coffee, breakfast (frijoles +
potatoes and a little 'goulash') and once again coffee, before the
line-up was ordered to start. Everyone had a justifiable burden.
My backpack was full of cans, plates, spoons and mugs, etc.,
and weighed about 15 kg.

At the last moment, of course, a tent was discovered, which
was forgotten and which must be included. The Chilotes were
fully loaded, and therefore they intended to start tearing the
load apart again to drop something less important than the
tent. But I thought that was unnecessary. I found a strap, fastened the tent bag on the outside of my backpack and started
climbing. The hike went well, although the 24 kilograms load
soon felt like 50. The route was not exactly a walking path, but
enough to be the first in Kelly Inlet.

Slowly we climbed up, slower than if I had been alone, for
the Professor is far too old to go on adventures like this. He is
tough and stubborn, but it does not help much, when he actu-
ally has to crawl on all fours. His sense of balance is right on
the limit. Where another person easily walks on his two feet, he
rushes forward on his 'stomach'. We took about three hours to
get up. For my part, I have to say, it did not look very promising
up there.

Today we have walked from 1 to X; there we pitched camp for the night; continued the following day to 2, where a more permanent camp was established. From there, Prof and Pallin intend to walk in the direction of the scratched area which inclines towards a tarn. From the other side of the mountain, we hope to see the San Tadeo Glacier. But I consider it unthinkable, although I did not want to say anything so as not to dampen the mood. The glacier is probably even further north. The two Chilotes and I left the others at the X and returned to the camp by the beach. Prof claimed that it would take at least two hours to get down here again, but that did not stop us from walking the route in a time of 30 minutes. But I think I'll take it a little slower next time, because it was risking my life too much. In any case, we are very safe.

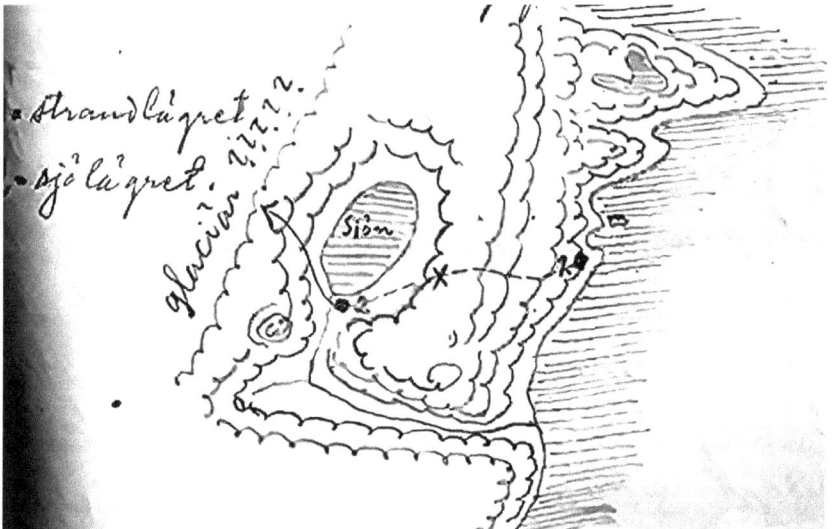

Allan's sketch of the route from Camp 1 to the tarn (Lago Steffen)

New Year's Day, 1921. Shortly after lunch, rice and potatoes and 'wing-herring' and coffee, I suddenly heard the Swedish language. It was the Professor and Pallin who returned. They had made an excursion from the lagoon camp to the top of the mountain, which obstructed the view to the north. When they got there, the San Tadeo Glacier was on the other side below them! So, there it was, the one eagerly sought!

But then the Professor got one of his crazy ideas. He wanted to reach the glacier another way. From the fjord camp, a route will be cut east to a valley, where a side glacier is located, and traversing it, make an advance towards the San Tadeo. This explains their rapid return. Rosen had stayed up in the lagoon camp, and I was ordered to pack immediately and with one of the men (i.e. one of the Chilotes) go up there for mapping. It was bumpy and heavy, the sweat flowed in streams, but we arrived after 1 ½ hours of climbing. And here I am sitting now. The dinner is just dehydrated rice + steak and coffee! Before the meal, I climbed a hill to orient myself and at the same time took the opportunity to set up a station sign.

Tomorrow the fun will begin. Now Rosen and I will see the sun go down and at the same time I will try to determine the compass's misalignment. There's a lot that a poor geographer may have in mind, but it's something magnificent, the science of God's glorious green earth. Now I start to freeze a little, because I became extremely sweaty during the climb.

Monday, 3ʳᵈ January 1921. I was careless with the 'diary' yesterday! But the cause was a little more than ordinary fatigue. According to the program, Rosen, the Chilote and I set off yesterday morning to climb 'Knallhatten'. A breakfast of a piece of smoked ham, a piece of bread, two plates of oatmeal and a few cups of coffee did not put more energy into the legs than was needed for the 65 m descent to the lagoon or 'Lago Steffen' (as it should be called). Then we had the whole 'Knallhatten' to climb. I carried the camera, the measuring table and its tripod, and sweated like a fireman at SJ[19]. But we received (as it is always called in mountaineering stories) ample reward for the effort.

Looking towards the north to Co Yañez and Laguna San Rafael in the far distance behind Co Yañez[20]

It was the most magnificent landscape of snow and ice and huge mountains I have ever seen. To the north we could see Laguna San Rafael with glaciers and swimming icebergs. To the west of it and towards us, a very slurry area spread, sacred and waterlogged, here and there intersected by glacial rivers. San Rafael and San Tadeo were separated by a mountain range, which ran east and west, but ended before reaching the coast. Between that and that mountain range, we saw the well-trodden San Tadeo Glacier, wide and mighty. Its 'Nährungsgebiet' (appearance[21]) seemed to be quite different from San Rafael's, and no trace of any ice sheet was visible. The glacier was of the alpine type. You could see the meridional (southern) mountain ridge to the east, from where larger and smaller glacier arms flowed west. Of course, I took photographs of the entire horizon. May they now be successful, for I need them for the map work.

So, I set up the measuring table, made in my 'angle book' some sketches of the landscape and drew some characteristic lines of sight. Then a sandwich with sardines and cheese was eaten, the pipe was lit, the meteorological observations were taken, and the journey home began. It went a little faster down-hill than uphill, but it was sweaty anyway. And you just did not get cooler from the climb from the lagoon up to the camp. There the food was put on immediately, rice with a little fruit and 'goulash'. When the sun promised to go down radiantly fine, I set up the theodolite to get a deviation determination (i.e. determination of the compass's misalignment in a certain place, using the shadow length or bearing to the sun and there-fore need cloudless weather), toiling with Rosen up on a hill to the west. But it did not happen. A cloud bank obscured today's setting sun just the moment it disappeared on the horizon. Well, à la bonheur, it was a handsome sunset anyway. Then we walked home. I tore off my outer wear and crawled drenched in sweat into my sleeping bag. The underwear I now wear is three weeks old. But they should stay on all the time!

Today, January 3, 1921, we started after breakfast for basic measurement down by the lagoon. I found 100 m. of decent terrain, measured it, set up the theodolite and took some angles. Meanwhile, Rosen strutted around and collected mos-quitoes. When I finished at 2 pm we climbed up to the camp and I immediately sat down to calculate my angles. Now it's ready, dinner has been eaten and it's time to go to bed. But the weather has become a bit dull again. It has been foggy all day. Now, in the afternoon, there has been a little drizzle. It would be a great pity if it rains tomorrow, because then I will do the measuring table work and need a break. If I have time to finish the survey tomorrow, we will start the evening for the 'beach camp'. Now I will at least sleep.

Goose family by Lago Steffen

Thursday, 6th January 1921. Thirteenth evening[22]. At the camp
at the San Tadeo Lake (Eagle Valley Camp). Once again I have
been careless with the story, and once again I am excused. It
has been extremely busy (then convoluted, hectic, much happened) the last few days. We have marched to the glacier. I last
wrote on 3rd January 1921. On the morning of the 4th, it was of
course foggy like oatmeal and a nice drizzle. I waited patiently
for a few hours but finally decided to go down into the valley with my measuring table, despite the rain. It was a test of
patience. I had not had time to set everything up before the
pouring rain came. Luckily, I had been foresighted enough to
bring a small piece of wax cloth, which was now placed on
the measuring table during the rain. And between the showers I worked and really managed to get together something
that looked like a map of the lagoon. So, I walked home at one

o'clock, got a cup of chocolate, sandwich and ham, after which Rosen and I held war councils and decided to return down to the beach camp that afternoon. We were about to start, when suddenly the Professor and Pallin appeared.

Their attempt to reach the glacier via 'Valley Road' had failed. Now all that remained was to climb over the mountains. They brought some of the equipment. The rest I would pick up in the beach camp. Rosen and I went with all the Chilotes down to the beach camp in the afternoon. Progress was fast and funny. The feet slipped out into the soaked moss and they went long distances to the stern saloon. After a ¾ hour march we arrived and started with food - frijoles, potatoes, corned beef, fruit soup, coffee and biscuits. I ate so much that I felt a little ill. Not exactly ill, but my stomach was as tense as the skin on a bass drum. I fell asleep, slept deeply and woke up like a 'roach' on 5th January at 8 am.

The packing and food tasks were soon finished, and at 11 am I started with our three Chilotes loaded, overloaded. Rosen was left alone in the camp to make collections and then observations during our absence. He does not have our interest in the glacier. We arrived at Camp 2 at 1 pm, got a cup of coffee and immediately started moving the position of the camp down the slope towards the lagoon. However, we did not collect everything, which is why the team left a tent at Camp 2. There were too many of us so we three 'men' climbed back to Camp 2, where we spent the night.

This morning we started the march up again to 'Knallhatten' and to the glacier. It was a very tough march, with heavy loads and my backpack was probably not so well packed. In addition, I had the common camera and the ice equipment[23]. But it went well. At the time of writing, we are in a small valley with

a pond (Shelf Lake) and from here we hope to be able to inter-
sect easily enough and obliquely to the glacier, which is a few
100 m below us. We return tomorrow to this lagoon camp No.
2 with the rest of the equipment. When we were left alone, we
started working on the tent and cooking. I cut a tent pole, collected firewood and started cooking. First a cup of chocolate,
sandwich and cheese. So, the macaroni was put on and after a
devilish toil with fire and stew I was finally able to serve macaroni, steak and coffee. Now everything is ready. In honour of
the thirteenth, Prof has distributed 4 (four) walnuts per man.
I lit one of Rosen's father's cigars (they were in the Christmas
box, but Rosen does not smoke cigars himself) and am now
sitting here at dusk.

Friday, 7th January 1921. The Lake Camp. I was up today at
6 am, peed and made a fire. But the former went better than
the latter. It took me an hour and a half to boil a coffee. So, the
porridge pan was put on. It was ready at 8. After the contents
were cooked, they were given to Prof and Pallin, who went off
to the glacier. I have stayed to guard the camp and receive the
Chilotes when they arrive. You cannot guess but it is calm and
peaceful here. Close by, a small stream is bubbling. In front of
me is the pond, pitch black, deep and magical. Around it rise
huge, bare, steep mountains. The sky is a little misty, but every
now and then the sun gets a chance to shine on me. Here we
have come up into the real mountain environment. The trees,
beeches and cypresses are low and twisted, the trunks look in
hooks and arches for the ground. The dead trunks stand white-
peeled and straight. Grass and mosses grow into a thick blanket where the moisture is greater, but flowers are rare and are
usually so small that they completely disappear in the moss.
There is a single larger flower here and I have added a few copies of it here in the book.

Saturday, 8th January 1921. The camp at the glacier. Finally, there! Finally, we are close to the San Tadeo Glacier, certainly one of the largest in the world and a very strange glacier in addition. Yesterday, Prof and Pallin returned from their reconnaissance trip at 2 o'clock. During their absence, the Chilotes had come from the lagoon camp with the rest of the equipment. After having eaten, they were sent down to the future glacier camp with a load of luggage. Prof followed them for a while on the way and when he returned, our dinner was eaten. So the rest of the day was wasted. The Chilotes stayed with us during the night. They slept in the open air, to finally help us down this morning. At 6 am I was on my feet, making coffee and waking the others. The packing was soon done,

Allan and Nils with tent at Eagle Valley Camp near the glacier

and after a 2 hour march in rough terrain with heavy loads, we were able to shed our burdens and designate space for the tent. It was erected on a moraine embankment, which the ice once built up.

The Chilotes received another instruction and were thanked with orders to pick us up on Saturday, 15 January. So, we were alone! The camp was fully prepared and so we started to look at the ice for a while. We climbed to the edge of the ice, put on the ladders (crampons) and tied ourselves together with the glacier rope. Pallin went first, Prof in the middle and I ended the 'queue'. It was not easy ice to get through. The crevasses were large and many. We immediately saw that there could be no talk of any extensive hikes. In addition, the ice was too heavy and our equipment too deficient. So, we returned to camp, and I started cooking. The wind blew strongly and since the fuel was also acidic, I did not succeed with the fire out in the open. I breathed heavily and swore but nothing helped. So, I grabbed the 'primus' and had to move the 'kitchen' into the tent. At first it went well. Dinner was over, and we all three sat inside the tent and waited for the coffee maker, which was on the 'primus'. Then things went wrong and, of course, the coffee maker fell in the lap of Prof. Of course, it was in a hurry, and the teacher became nervous like a hen, ran here and there and everywhere. The whole thing was a trifle, confined to a little water on his sleeping bag, which did not even wet through the cover. But no matter how insignificant the matter was, it was large enough to create discontent in the camp. I was angry as a bee. Why I certainly do not know, and crawled as soon as possible into the sleeping bag, pulled the hood over my head, and tried to fall asleep. However, sleep has not materialised.

Nils and Allan on San Tadeo Glacier

After a while I crawled out again, looked for the diary and here I am now! The program for tomorrow is large and extensive; we have planned a long three-day ice trek east.

✧

Chapter 5

FIRST OF ALL AT THE GIANT GLACIER

by Nils Pallin

Professor Nordenskjöld in front of the San Tadeo Glacier

During the time of our transfer to the ice, you can almost say that we had had summer. In any case it was the only summer that we got to know in Patagonia. It rained comparatively little, and one morning in Camp 1, even cobwebs had been formed in the rain gauge during the night. This weather with no rain came in useful for the arduous transfer, but it would have been even better if we had got it on the ice, because after arriving there, any semblance of fair weather ceased.

At the camp in Eagle Valley, we lived as the first people in a new and captivating world. From our little tent on the moraine's grassy south side, we had a mirrored view of the small Warm Tarn with the 'Big Top' straight in the background, the Waterfall Valley's needle-sharp ridge to the west and situated high up the shelf of the Rock Tarn on the right side, all in an impressive majesty. Straight down into the tarn in the centre of the valley there was the steeply falling Eagle Rock, on whose monumental peak our two eagles used to sit. When the storm did not roar around the mountain peaks, you could hear the Rock Tarn stream roar like an airplane from the upper parts of the valley, without it being possible to detect its outlet in Warm Tarn.

If you climbed to the top of the moraine and glanced over its border to the north, immediately below the moraine's gravelly outside, you saw the small glacial lake with the San Tadeo Glacier's white ice wall, about 40 metres high, ascending vertically from the water, obstructing all view. Its crevasses ran almost parallel to the wall, occasionally causing huge plates of thick glacier ice to be peeled off into the lake, where the ice calves drifted around in the wind in large blocks. The camp was situated at a height of 325 metres above sea level. To a sharply marked height of another 25 metres, all growing forest had disappeared. But above this boundary the rainforest ascended towards the heights until it was halted by the vertical slopes, or the rising altitude above the sea. Apparently, the glacier had previously been greater in height and extent than now, as this lower forest boundary was in fact a shoreline[01]. Extinct trees were seen in many places in the narrow basin area and next to the edge of the warm tarn was a still quite healthy beech trunk, no less than three metres in circumference. Judging from this and other signs, the Tadeo Glacier has been through big changes.

San Tadeo Glacier looking north-west with Nils Pallin.
In the foreground is Warm Tarn and in the background is Glacier Lake[02]

From here, we would penetrate further over the ice and complete our investigations. But this was more easily said than done, because we had to fight all the powers of the vault of heaven. The day after our arrival the rain began with a vengeance, and it was not long before we understood that we no longer had any mercy to expect from the climate. The moments when it was not raining were easily counted both in number and length. And it rained perfectly immoderate. Worse rainstorms I have never been able to dream of. Although the ridge of the moraine, inside of which the tent was pitched, was no further away than five to ten metres, it collected so much rainwater that we had to dig ditches around the tent with the axe to divert the water. In the warm tarn, on the other side of the tent, the water rose several times so high, that it threatened to enter the tent. In this we had to lie with raincoats and sou'-westers on, and for several days it was impossible to stick your nose outside the tent slot. Everything rainproof, all rain clothes and tents, became frayed by the eternal raining, so that finally both tents and oil garments were like sieves. Everywhere the noisy, indescribably dry and tantalizing croaking of the frogs spoke in clear language about the creatures for which this climate was created. A lone bird that repeated its frail double chirp ten to fifteen times in a row, was the only encouraging and bright spot in this miserable nature.

If we previously had found the conditions difficult in our coastal camp at the Kelly Fjord, here we had to endure the utmost of what an abandoned existence can offer of nastiness and anguish. Days and nights went by in a terrible monotony. We lay in the narrow four-piece army tent, crawled in our damp sleeping bags between our contraptions stacked together, smoked our pipes and listened to the thunder from the glacier, while we discussed scientific problems or cooked our food. The cooking had to be done on the primus and inside the tent, as it was impossible to keep a fire in the open.

Even those wizards at fire fixing, our Chilotes, failed one night when they had returned with additional food supplies and had to camp outdoors during the long night in torrential rain. Poor devils! For any tougher, more persevering, contented and cheerful people you would have to look far. Often, when I saw them in their hard lives and trips in all weathers, with joy in living their primitive, miserable existence, I could not avoid making comparisons with the advanced, delicate and unsatisfied cultivated flowers we have become ourselves. Is it from them to us that a true and noble, world improving development should go? That we and our actions were a mystery to them is easy to understand. As far as we understood them right, they thought that we were looking for gold, and they found herein a good explanation for our, in their eyes, furious desire to overwhelm ourselves with difficulties[03].

But it was not only the climate that was unfavourable for us. Even here obstacles would meet us in unexpected ways. Like how the expedition at the Kelly Fjord was stopped by the sandbanks that the glacier streams had deposited almost everywhere, our freedom of movement on the Tadeo Glacier would be halted by wild crevasse zones that were crossing through the ice[04] in all directions. These crevasse formations start mainly at such points where a disturbance occurs in the normal course of the glacier, usually due to irregular shapes in the valley sides where the glacier flows. They arise especially at the points where side valleys enter into the glacier valley, and where the ice gets sucked into the side valleys, and makes the glacier expand in width and open larger or smaller longitudinal crevasses. When the ice slides past a crossing valley and blocks its mouth with its dam, it collects the water that flows in the valley behind this dam. In this way the ice dammed lakes arise, of which we have a small but beautiful example below our camp. Through the movements of the ice, occasionally transverse crevasses also occur in the damming ice wall, whereby the water may suddenly completely or partly run off, so that the lake disappears. When the crevasses then re-join, the water gets dammed up again, and the lake is resurrected.

One of the glacier-dammed lakes[05]

On our advancement along the Tadeo Glacier's banks, we repeatedly encountered these lakes. They gave us the alternative to either make a long detour around the lake into the surrounding rainforest, or to hazard out on the violently cracked and broken ice outside the side valley. The former was usually futile and the latter forced us to long detours out on the glacier, whose surface further out in some places could be fairly smooth and easy going. In this way, despite the rain we made long excursions on the ice through all weathers and over endless moraine fields, which like thin gravel and stone cloth covered the glacier's surface, or over the rain-washed ice fields between gaps and banks of ice, which twisted like sleeping creatures in horrible nightmares.

On the ice of San Tadeo Glacier looking further east

Down towards the sea near the glacier tongue a promontory reached out into the glacial ice. In the lee of the dead water or 'dead ice' under this promontory, the glacier was completely covered by this above-mentioned moraine field, that appears like a dirty layer against other parts of the glacier. By this 'Dirt Cape' that, as we had already observed from the sea, the glacier made a violent leap down towards the coast and closed the route to the tongue with an insurmountable immense ice-fall[06].

Near the terminus of San Tadeo Glacier looking east

The first time we went on a trip in this direction, our route had been closed by an ice-dammed lake. It reached far out into the side valley and had its mouth there. But a few days later when we returned to the same place, the water was almost drained and only a small lagoon remained in a deep bowl near the ice edge. Big blocks of ice had been stranded on the dry bottom which lacked side moraines. We were able to pass this obstacle, which nature itself had so quickly removed, by a slight detour. On the other side it was easy to get up on the ice to avoid the extremely blocky and hard walked glacial shore, on which the ice edge generally finished like tortoise shields. But in places the ice had fallen down in colossal piles of ice blocks. We could then walk on the smooth and crevasse-free ice, striped with different annual layers, all the way to the ice-fall at 'Dirt Cape'. There we were given a general view of the glacier's tongue and its foreland by the coast, outside of which the Golfo de Penas rolled its roaring breakers. Here we could also hastily finish our measurements and then instead concentrate

on the most important of all, the source areas of the glacier, in
the Cordilleras to the east.

Stranded blocks of ice from a drained lake

*Southern edge of San Tadeo Glacier looking towards the east
with moraine in foreground[06] [AJ]*

From the glacier ascended several 'nunataks' (rock islands), all more or less overgrown with forest. On the north side of glacier rose the high mountainous land between the Tadeo Glacier and the Rafael Glacier. To the east, the glacier stretched with incalculable fields up towards the Cordilleras, whose peaks now and then glimpsed through rain mists over the boundary contours of the ice. The glacier shore on which we were, ended up to the east by a double top mountain of the same type as 'the Bowler', located in the very angle between the Tadeo Glacier and the Kelly Glacier.

On our journey eastwards, we were soon stopped by a lake, elongated, deeply cut, surrounded by forest and ice-dammed - Lago Bäckman. To walk around it with the resources that were available to us at the ice camp was unthinkable. In addition, this side valley had attracted the glacier ice so strongly that it was torn apart in the most violent way outside the valley. We had already been able to observe this when we climbed the 'Big Top', and from there we had also noted that the ice higher up, thanks to the ice branch deviating from the Tadeo Glacier and culminating in the Kelly Valley, was impassable because of its huge crevasse areas. The entire glacier in this direction looked like fields of countless pointed pyramids, with innumerable gaps and crevasses. Unfortunately, a step-by-step advancement with tents over this ice was impossible. Above this area the steep ice-falls came rolling over and down from the mountains, initially in the form of local branches, enclosing dark rock islands. Above those associated ice-falls was the vast unbroken ice armour which covers the watershed between the two oceans. From these expeditions we made clear to ourselves the ice distribution and the nature of the visible area.

But to complement the picture in the closer area, we had to make a thrust also into the inner part of the Kelly Fjord.

Much of the time of the stay at the Tadeo Glacier was not useful for investigations, because the rain constantly flowed in streams. No man could stand roaming about totally wet in the long run, with unusable scientific equipment, without doing anything useful, and only from pure ambition. Most evenings we could therefore look back on unrewarding days, and when we put out the lantern with the rain splashing on the tent, the only thing to do was to take it easy and let the weather have its time.

The neighbourhood around the camp, however, was thoroughly investigated, though. There was *one* particular problem that occupied our imagination.

In the immediate vicinity of our tents, the uniform plain moraine descended and formed like a gate in the wall. In front of this opening in the valley, some violent intervention had apparently taken place. Large and small stones were thrown around over the grassy ground, and mighty platforms of turf were peeled up, or thrown around or turned upside down, seemingly in aimless disorder[07]. A burst of pebbles had ended right out in the Warm Tarn, out there resembling the island groups in the Pacific Ocean. That the incident which caused this disaster was recent became apparent because the grass and the sprigs on the upside-down turned twigs were green and ripe berries could be picked on their pernettya-sprigs. We troubled our brains several times over this phenomenon, and various rationales for it were tested. Among other theories one came up that what we saw were traces of activity by some prehistorical animal, whose existence people may have found reasons to assume lived in these deserted regions of Patagonia in earlier times. It would have been a nasty business, if any such archaic giant revealed itself to us here. We were unarmed and without protection against attacks of this kind.

However, we had no fear, because these theories are too improbable to be taken seriously. If they contained any grain of truth, we would of course also on other points have seen traces of these monsters. But the question was difficult enough. To clarify it, I made an accurate measurement of the field one day when I stayed in the camp to repair shoes, and plotted the disaster details on a map. After studying this, there seemed to be no more than one basis for explanation. An immense ice block or perhaps an entire ice cliff must have fallen at once from the glacier. By its fall into the lake, it started huge waves, concentrated towards the opening in the moraine, smashed this and flung the scattered material, probably for the most part stemming from the partially broken moraine edge. As simple as this explanation may seem, it was with this riddle as with so many other scientific problems. They all take their time to solve. In Darwin's description of his journey around the Earth, he mentions a similar case in that at one point on the Beagle Channel shores in the Terra del Fuego, he saw large boulders being moved due to surge waves from a glacier collapse.

Finally, after two weeks of staying by and on the Tadeo Glacier, we were forced by the terrible rain to return. This was done with no regrets. Our return home would have been a pure pleasure, if fate had not just then wanted to give us a final, eruptive, personal experience of what that neighbourhood could perform at its best or worst in the form of rain. When we were breaking up to return, a fairly gentle rain fell. But well on our way, the storm began to howl and the rain to fall, as if the windows of heaven were open and all its angels weeping over the wickedness of the world from time immemorial. From the very steep walls of the valley flowed broad, roaring, white ribbons of streams, of whose existence we previously had no idea. It was as if numerous flame throwers with burning zeal exhausted their contents over the Earth. In the mountains, the fog was thick as a jet of steam, whipping wet and permeating cold. It became in many ways a record day in roughness. The simplest way to sum up the day was to measure the rainfall, which was more than a hundred millimetres, falling with constant force during a violent storm.

How do you say in Sweden, when you have been out there in unusually lousy weather? You shake your head and snort from between pale blue lips. Shame for the Evil One! But no hard words could help us here, and we were hardened men. Instead, we raised a real sigh of relief when we finally passed over the watershed on the way southwards and were going downwards again towards the Kelly Fjord. There we had many tents and various changes of clothes. It was for all of us a true 'reinvigoration', that in a rainy grey and a more than usually gloomy twilight we saw our coastal camp again. We knocked back a hot drink by the flickering candle flames, which reminded us that the days were already beginning to get shorter, and that autumn was approaching with rapid strides.

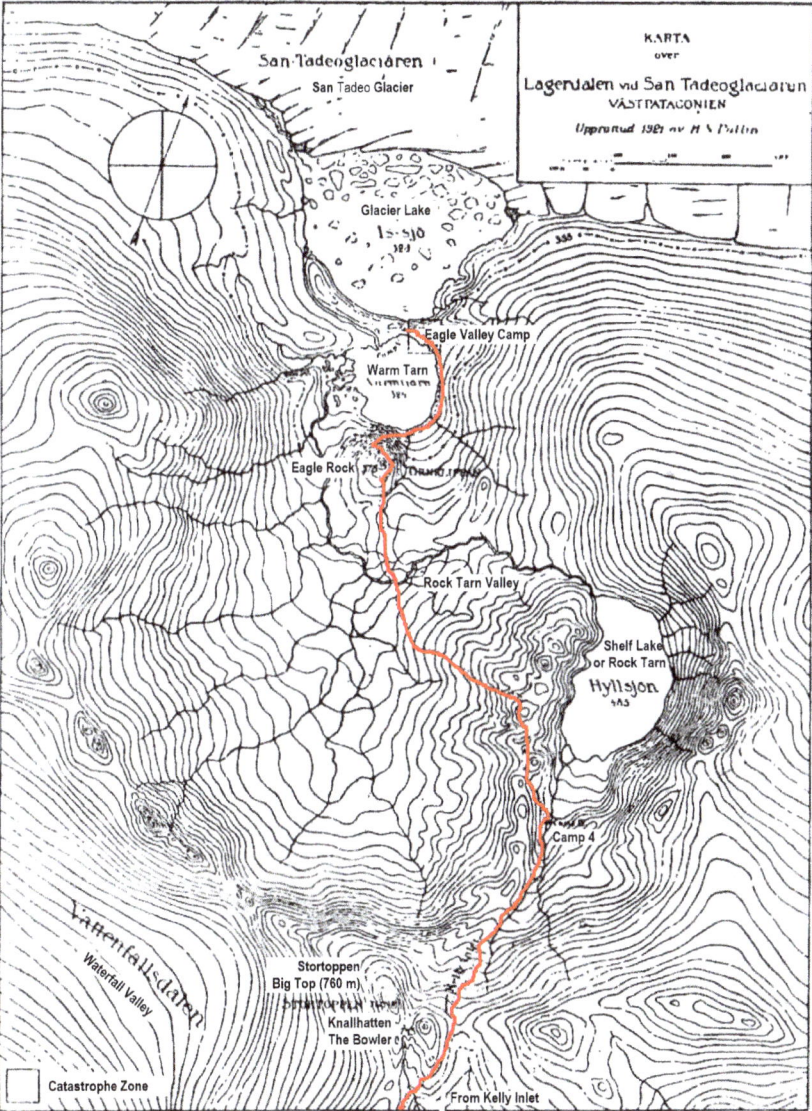

Nils Pallin's map of Eagle Valley to the edge of San Tadeo Glacier [AJ][08]

Extracts from Allan Bäckman's Letters

Sunday, 9th January 1921. The camp at the glacier. Even today I am in the camp by the glacier, because the day is rainy. Already last night, the weather turned out to be a bit rainy. Last night a few millimetres fell, but when I got up at 6 o'clock to turn on the coffee it was intermittent weather. At 7 o'clock the food, coffee and oatmeal were ready. But then we had so much rain that there could be no talk of an ice walk. The barometer fell at an incredible speed and from the north came heavy rain clouds. Therefore, we decided to limit ourselves to a small trip up on the cliff east of the camp valley. I loaded the backpack full of instruments for mapping. It probably became too heavy. The other two expeditioners carried nothing. But despite that, they got tired after we climbed up a quarter of an hour. Prof blamed that he had nothing to do up there. Pallin suddenly remembered that he had seen a lot of interesting things by the small moraine-dammed lake next to the camp. He considered it appropriate to take a closer look at it today. Then they wandered down, and I continued my climb alone. It was rough enough, but I was up after half an hour of work.

Then it turned out that I had come up on a forestless mountain ridge, which went east. I followed it as far as I could and got to see a lot of interesting things. Among other things it turned out impossible to pass the ice to the east, so our plan for an ice hike in that direction must be scrapped. I found a large valley lake dammed by ice (Lago Bäckman), which we had not had the slightest idea about before. Despite pouring rain, I set up the prismatic compass and got some aiming lines, enough for a map sketch. But at one of my target stations, the rain became too heavy and also a misty north wind blew. I crawled into the shelter behind a rock, lit the pipe and began to think.

So, the journey home began. I went wrong twice, came to the vertical rock wall and had to look for a new way. Meanwhile the rain poured down, the wet branches whipped me in the face. Most of the time I slipped, slipped on the 'tail' (da butt) for long stretches in the wet moss and was consequently wet as a cod on the bare body, when I arrived at the camp at 1 pm. Then the Professor was in the tent preparing the food, rice and fried pork. I crawled into the tent, pulled off one pair of the soaked socks and felt satisfied with my work.

Lago Bäckman[09]

Although the clothes are damp, it is necessary to let them dry on the body here. Otherwise, they do not dry at all. It's a bit chilly, but it has to work. The rest of the day has been spent in the tent talking, writing and smoking. It's a little sad, but we hope for better weather tomorrow. Now the steak is fried, I have to assist!

Tuesday, 11ᵗʰ January 1921. The camp by the glacier. Yesterday was the saddest expedition day so far. Already yesterday it rained, as described and yesterday morning, vivid torrential rain and an incredible north wind blew up. The wind came rushing over the glacier, rolled over the moraine and fell over our small tent with hurricane-like strength. The canvas fluttered and slammed, stood tense like an umbrella and threatened to go over the pond every moment. The rain was beating through the canvas. Crouched in our sleeping bags we heard the regular splash, splash, as the big drops of heavy rain fell against our belongings and soaked everything. The only thing we could do was cook food on the primus and sleep. We did not dare to 'pee' but used a can as a necessity vessel and then threw out the contents through the door slot. You probably understand that the mood was not very high, I absolutely did not want to write anything.

And today is about the same as yesterday, however, the storm has calmed down a bit and there is a little break between showers. Now (at 12 noon) coffee will be boiled, and we hope to work outside for a few minutes this afternoon.

At 2:55 the same day. Now the Professor has travelled in advance to see what the west route looks like. My reconnaissance the day before yesterday made it clear that to the east we cannot hope to advance. If we cannot go west either, well then we sit as if in a trap and have to content ourselves with waiting until we are picked up. By the way, the weather is as disgusting as it may be. It promised to clear at noon, but now the rain is pounding against the canvas again. I have not made a creative meal today. I boiled a delicious oat meal, fried nine pieces of pork and cooked the most 'delightful' sip of coffee, which has so far been enjoyed by the Nordenskjöld South American expedition.

This has been my task for the day. In addition, I took a photo. In doing so, I discovered that my broken visor (matte board for camera) was an excellent mirror. I naturally spent half an hour looking at and admiring my masculine features, which are now further beautified by a stately, raven-black full beard. I have serious thoughts about keeping it, until I come 'back to the mother Earth'. Personal hygiene is a bit neglected. I have not washed since New Year's Eve, nor brushed my teeth since. But I take good care of my nails, because I trim them every week. By the way, I do not have time to get dirt on my hands as the grease always goes off when cooking and especially when washing dishes.

It is quite strange that health is so lagging behind in these disgusting living conditions. If I just went as wet as now one day at home, I bet 10 against 1 that staggering pneumonia would be the result. Now I have practically been soaked ever since December 20th. In the beginning, the nose ran slightly, but it is tired of it. I am healthy and strong as a horse, toil sweaty and warm on the mountain sides, crawl through into the tent and let the clothes dry on my body . All this in a temperature of about 7 to 8 degrees above zero.

I brought a pair of powder-dry shoes in my backpack here to the glacier camp, and I was overjoyed to get something dry on my feet at some point. Last night I picked them up, put them in what I thought was good protection during the night. In the morning they were full of water. The rain had beaten through the tent during the night, and the drops had eventually filled my shoes, which stood with the shafts opening upwards. You probably understand that I did not just read the psalm verse when I discovered the situation! But there was nothing to do but put on the misery (of sodden shoes), and after my feet had cooled down to lumps of ice, I just did not notice the discomfort. Now this is as much as I can write today. The rice should be boiled, and then I will take some photos, if the sun emerges for a second.

Saturday, 15th January 1921. The camp by the glacier. But now I'm once so pompous that I like to be lazy, especially when it comes to small things. Therefore, today it is 15th January, and I have not recorded anything since the 11th. As I then wrote, Prof and Pallin went out in the rainy weather on 11th to the west to look around. They managed to see a small icy lake in a valley. Of course, they wanted to upset me. This lake was the topic of conversation in the evening. On 12th January, it was raining. There was a short break in the rain at 2 o'clock, so I then went outside and measured an 86-m-long baseline for the map. No more was done that day.

On 13th January, we made our first major hike west. The weather looked promising as well, at least somewhat so when I woke up at 6:30. When I saw that Prof also was awake, did I make an inquiry, if I should put in ???? with the food. This request, however, was answered in the negative as we were in no hurry. Which, moreover, was clearly demonstrated by the fact that we did not leave until 10 am. It was a hell of a climb on the huge side moraine, which constantly accompanies the glacier. The latter is too crevasse-filled to be used as a country road. I stayed at a couple of clearly visible points and took some angles for the mapping. Of course, Prof, I imagined, wanted the wonderful opportunity for mapping and I persuaded myself to bring a measuring table + stand. This is why my backpack was heavy as lead. I was not allowed to use the measuring table once that day. It only served to make me sweaty and angry. When we arrived at their much-talked-about ice lake, it turned out that it had shrunk to an insignificant amount. It was being emptied by some kind of drain hidden by the ice. So, we continued for a while on the moraine, finally took on the ice and entered the glacier, which now formed a relatively crevasse-free surface. Our goal was a headland, which was named Smutsudden (the 'Dirt Cape') after its incredible sand and moraine accumulations. We did not reach it, however, because huge crevasses prevented it.

The drained 'lake'

I saw very well where we could have managed the route. But as I am considered the novice when it comes to ice hiking and glaciers, I did not voice my opinion. The result was that we went down the moraine again, a job that took us 1.5 hours, as the descent was to take place 'according to all the rules of art' with stair cutting etc. I smiled really well. If I had been alone I would have simply crouched down with the ice axe between

my legs and thus gone 'kana' down. It would have been completely harmless and taken a minute.

After 1½ hours of hard work we had carved out 12 to 15 steps
in the ice. It turned out to be impossible to continue along the
moraine as well. All that remained was to seek out the forest,
which covered a hillside, to get an overview of the landscape
to the west. We did not succeed in this either. We got stuck
in a bog and no one got anywhere. So, the retreat began, not
quite as proud as the advance. The day was an absolute failure.
Darkness fell quickly. During the last half hour I had quite a
hard time seeing where it was appropriate to set foot. At 8:40
pm I arrived at the tent, turned on the light and primus and
started the kitchen task. After the meal, I changed plates in the
camera and crawled into the sleeping bag.

Roping off the moraine-clad glacier side

The next morning, 14th January (yesterday) started with a small problem. Pallin did not want to follow on a second attempt to reach Smutsudden ('Cape Dirt'). He blamed broken shoes, but . . . . Well, there was nothing left but for Prof and I to travel alone. At 10 in the morning, we set off and at 2 we arrived at Smutsudden, which we reached by ice. When it turned out that the view over the glacier tongue and its foreland to the west was not as first-class as desired, we decided to climb up to the same height as yesterday.

Smutsudden ('Dirt Cape') with some of the glacier tongue in the distance

At least now I decided the ascent point and after two hours of stiff climbing we were up. I have never seen something so magnificent and will probably never see it again. The entire San Tadeo Glacier was widespread in front of us. To the west the sea glistened between the Taitao Peninsula protrusion. Far to the north we glimpsed San Rafael lake and glacier. Beyond, Seno Elefantes was enclosed between soaring distant blue mountains. To the east, the jagged, snow-white outline of the watershed mountain range loomed. It was unforgettable!

Unfortunately, I had been forced to leave my camera at the foot of the mountain, so difficult was the ascent. After a few brief notes, we have to go again start toiling. After half an hour of 'canoeing' down the hillside, we were able to climb the glacier again and now we went quickly home. Pallin was waiting there. During the day he had partly mapped the valley, in which we are located. In addition, the Chilotes had brought food from the main station. But dinner was not cooked. Dead tired, soaked (the last hour had rained down from east) and angry like a bee, I had to sit by the pot myself. At 11 o'clock, everything was ready, I changed camera plates again, and crawled into the sleeping bag.

Accessing the glacier

Nils Pallin surveying by Warm Tarn

In a while, Prof and I head east and tomorrow the journey home to the main station begins! Hurray!

—

Allan standing on recently exposed moraine material[10]

At 4:05 pm the same day! We did not get very far on our ice walk, the Professor and me. We put on the ladders (crampons), tied ourselves together with ropes and climbed with the help of the ice axes up an ice slope. Once there, we could not walk more than about 300 m into the glacier before the ice crevasses definitely said stop. We stopped for a while for photography and mapping, then the return march began. Once 'ashore' we decided to seek out the ice-dammed lake I discovered (and which I named 'Laguna Elna' in silence[11]). It was a little awkward trip, but soon we were up on a small hill at the mouth of the lagoon, and the Professor congratulated me on having seen the magnificent landscape first of all. I took some photos (see Lago Bäckman above), did some sightseeing and then we returned to the camp, where we arrived at 2 o'clock. Then the rice was cooked. Along with a jar of 'corned beef' it made for an excellent dinner accompanied by coffee and biscuits. Now we've digested the food for a while, Pallin's busy making a little special map. Prof is going out right now to look at the ice, and I'm sitting here writing.

View of the southern edge of San Tadeo Glacier with 'Dirt Cape', a slight smudge in the distance. Glacier altitude ranges from 350 m to 250 m. Warm Tarn is in the first valley on the left

On calmer and more sensible reflection I have always acknowledged that this journey has been of immense importance to me. I have seen with my own eyes most of what I have only read about before. Geography has come alive for me through this journey, and with fresh courage I will, when I return home, embark on an in-depth study of the glorious science.

Monday, 17th January 1921. There was nothing to do on the 16th with the home march delayed. It was raining inside (the tent). All day the rain was so hard it was like a rod in the ground, and we had to stay in our sleeping bags. It was so hard hour after hour that the drops drummed on the tent cloth. Eventually it got soaked too and then it rained in the tent as well. The moisture in the ground became so great that it penetrated into the sleeping bags from below (we had no tent floor), and after a few hours I was wet as a dishcloth. The night has not been pleasant under such conditions; I have been awake most of the night, for I froze about my naked neck. This morning there was no improvement in the weather, hail showers for a change to the rain showers. I had absolutely no desire to crawl out into the rain to pick up the food and kitchen materials. Consequently our breakfast consisted of 9 sardines (per person) on a 'sextant[12]', a small glass of cognac and several pipes of smoke.

Towards 11 o'clock it got a little better. The clouds began to fade, and the sun emerged from time to time. The breakfast (the second one) was prepared, rice + fried pork, coffee and several pipes of smoke. The weather invited photography, and I took the opportunity to take five photos. Pallin has now gone up on 'Örnberget' (Eagle Mountain) to complete his special map. Prof shall look below at the ice lagoon, and therefore I reside alone here for a while. We wait for the Chilotes back here tonight or tomorrow, and then we have to march home no matter what the weather, because the food supply has reduced alarmingly. It will probably be tricky to go home over the mountains in one day. Now I also long intensely for orderly, calm and more comfortable conditions down at the station.

Wednesday, 19th January 1921. The camp by the fjord shore! We lay by the glacier and waited for the Chilotes to start the home march. But the men did not come, and we waited for them in vain yesterday morning. It was already raining lightly when we woke up and the rain increased in intensity as did the north wind every minute. Despite that, we decided to go on our own. The food was soon ready, the personal stuff was packed in the backpacks, the rest was stuffed in bags and made completely ready to be picked up by the Chilotes. But when everything is ready, the Professor, as always, wanted to wait 'a quarter of an hour to see if the weather would improve'. Which it did not. So why we did not leave before 11 o'clock in the morning? Then the rain poured down. From the wind we did not feel much, as long as we were down in the valley. But from the furious speed of the clouds enshrouding the mountain tops I guessed what awaited us up there.

After 2 hours of strenuous climbing, we finally reached our penultimate campsite by the Rock Tarn (Shelf Lake). Then I was absolutely wet. Due to the climb, I could not use my long oil coat but had put my windbreaker on top of the leather vest. But these garments did not keep out the moisture, nor did my broken shoes and riding breeches. I cannot say that it is nice to climb in mountain areas soaked in pouring rain, in hurricane-like winds and in +4 degrees temperature. Also, the fog had thickened, so we could not see more than 20 meters in front of us. However, fog had hitherto not caused us any discomfort, as we knew the route we had walked a couple of times. But when we sought our way up from the Rock Tarn valley past Stortoppen (the Big Top) and Knallhatten down to 'Laguna Steffen', then it would get worse.

The fog absolutely prevented us from any orientation and the eternal rain created a maze of small lakes and streams, which were absolutely unfamiliar and confused us. We were left standing there without the opportunity to continue. A short war council! Pallin suggested a return march; he did not want to risk his life in the fog in the mountains. The Professor said he would wait for a while 'to see if the weather did not improve'. But since one could not stand still without freezing to ice, his proposal could be rejected immediately. I did not speak in the meeting, but when it turned out how difficult it was to find my way back to Klipptjärnsdalen (Rock Tarn Valley), even though we were not more than a hundred meters from it, I made a decision.

I asked if the others were determined to return to the starting camp, which was confirmed. So, I asked, if Prof as leader forbade me to continue alone over the mountains to the Base Station camp. He did not forbid me, said neither yes nor no. But Pallin dissented, which did not change my decision. I relieved, in Pallin's presence, the Professor of all responsibility for my life, shook hands with them, and after a few seconds the fog had separated us. They returned to the camp at the glacier, and I began the hike over the mountains to the Base Station camp. Did I do the right thing? Did I do the right thing against Prof and Pallin? That was the first question. When I left them, they were standing on the pass to Klipptjärnsdalen and had to walk a road, which they had walked four times before. In addition, they were two and could thus help each other in tricky situations. As we went up the route in two hours, they should not need more time to go down. The danger that they would be forced to spend the night in the open air was not great. Down in the camp they had food and sleeping bags. When I took all this into account, I did not consider myself in any way to increase the danger they were in if I left them. But then came the second question. Did I do the right thing?

That I risked my life was clear. The fog was thicker than ever. I did not know for sure where I was. I had only a clue where

I was going to go. The danger of getting lost was thus great and increased by the really awful mountain nature with vertical abysses and soaked moss. It may seem as if it was pure and simple folly of me to risk my life, but I still had my reasons. First of all, I was absolutely soaked, every thread on my body was soaked. If I went back, I would have to spend the night, albeit in tents but equally soaked, as I did not have dry clothes to change into. My sleeping bag was also soaked with water, which had penetrated into the tent. That is, the prospects for a first-class cold were as great as possible. If, on the other hand, I managed to get down to the Station camp, I had dry clothes, a dry sleeping bag, food, coffee and alcohol in abundance.

In addition, we had already walked in my opinion the most difficult part of the road. I need only glimpse Knallhatten for a second, so I could instantly orient myself and thus all danger would be over. Finally, I was young and strong, my muscles were in full training and I even dare to say that in my ability to get ahead in mountain terrain I could fully measure myself with Pallin. And so, I finally asked myself: 'Am I doing the right thing?' So, I made a decision, said, as mentioned, goodbye to the others and walked on.

When the fog parted us, I paused for a moment. In front of me I glimpsed some rock walls, which fell down vertically towards a valley hidden by the fog. It must be the valley east of Stortoppen, so I will keep to the right, seek my way up the mountain wall, seek to reach Stortoppen and from there follow the edge to Knallhatten. I went slowly uphill. At each step I sought support with my ice axe, carefully selected each place where I put my foot and moved carefully with the heavy backpack so as not to lose balance. Despite all the caution, I slipped in the wet moss most of the time, but it was not something serious. I eventually came up to the top of the mountain, but there I encountered a new difficulty. I had never been up on Stortoppen and consequently did not recognize my location up there. It all seemed a little unpleasant, and I gradually began to wonder if it would not have been wiser to follow the others. Then the fog eased for a few seconds and in front of me I glimpsed Knallhatten's characteristic contour! All right! Now I knew my way. I climbed carefully on the ridge towards Knallhatten. With the storm all around me, I had to seek support several times from rocks and boulders so as not to blow over.

Eventually, however, I came up on Knallhatten, looking right at the cairn that Prof and Pallin built there, and so I was sure of my position. But nonetheless, I went wrong on the last descent, came out onto a steep mountain side and had to climb to the top once more to be able to orientate myself. It was a difficult climb. I was already dead tired. The wind cooled my wet clothes and despite all my efforts my teeth chattered from the cold. After diligently searching for more than an hour, I finally found the way down and all danger was over. However, I took it all a little too casually, because suddenly I lost my footing and started sliding downhill. The speed grew, my feet found no support in the wet moss and it all turned out a little unpleasant, when the ice axe finally saved me. It got stuck between a couple of rocks, and a second later I was standing firmly on my feet again. The incident warned me and I regained my careful climbing. Then the wind suddenly turned to the south, tore off the fog and the road was clear and clear in front of me. I hurried. After half an hour I was down at 'Laguna Steffen'. I looked up to the old camp site and exhaled. Now nothing could stop me further. I only had to follow the cut road in the forest. In an hour or so I would be in the station. I ate my sandwiches, a box of sardines, and resumed the march.

Soon I glimpsed the tents, saw the smoke from the camp-fire, and rejoiced. When I arrived, I immediately picked out dry clothes, pulled on the big sweater and crawled into the sleeping bag. Then a large pot of hot coffee was brought to me. I filled my mug with half coffee and half cognac. I drank three such mugs. After a while I got potatoes and steak, more coffee and cognac, and a mug of currant brandy. I crept all the way into the sleeping bag. After about an hour I woke up again, found that I was dripping with sweat and fell asleep peacefully. Today I am in full vigour again, but when it is raining and I can do nothing, I am still in my sleeping bag.

At 6 o'clock the Chilotes left here to help Prof and Pallin. The weather yesterday must have been worse than usual, because the Chilotes intended to cross the mountains to the glacier but were forced to turn around. Which increases my gratitude for the providence, which helped me forward, where not even the Chilotes dared to advance, even though they were three in company.

✧

Chapter 6

THE JOB IS DONE

by Nils Pallin

Inner part of Kelly Inlet with the Kelly Glacier (Glacier Andrée) [AJ][01]

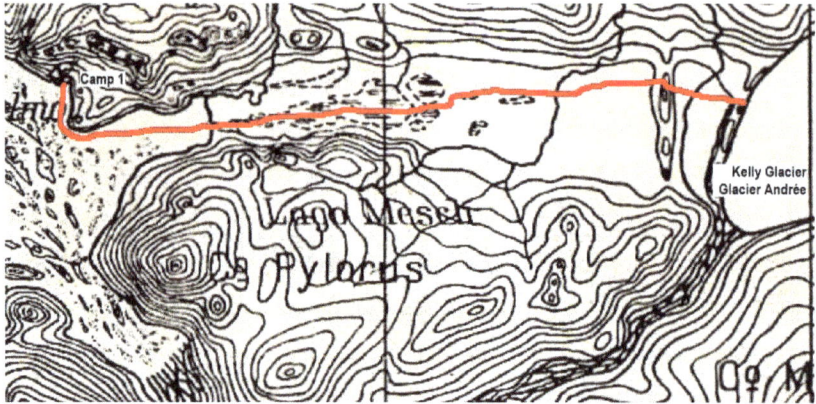

The route to the Kelly Glacier [AJ]

We returned to the coast camp on 19th January 1921. The task now left to complete was to as soon as possible try to advance to the Kelly Glacier, i.e. to the glacier which descends into the northern of the two major bays of the fjord, and which, according to the observances made by us, was a delta branch of the Tadeo Glacier. On 1st February, we were supposed to be picked up by a government steamer, and thus time was short. Another circumstance that made the pause in the camp short was the tide. As I previously mentioned, the whole Kelly Fjord as far as to some distance outside the Boscosa Islands is filled with glacial sludge that prevents forward advancement by boat, except once in a month by spring tide. It is possible to get through in certain directions by studying beforehand at low tide the extremely tangled drainage systems between the sludge banks. Right on our return from the Tadeo Glacier, a spring tide was approaching, and we had only one day to prepare for this, our new excursion. When this was done, however, we were stopped in the camp for two days by the rain, and therefore could not start until the evening of 22nd January, when the tide was fortunately still high enough to let us in our heavily loaded boat pass the critical banks by the Harbour Isthmus.

The mud flats of Kelly Inlet[02]

Dead trees on the way to the Kelly Glacier

We rowed into the bay that the Kelly Fjord formed within this headland in the shadow of Pylorus. Under whose dark silhouette a sharp line appeared in the Fjord between the light, dirty grey water from the South Glacier's branches and the dark moss-coloured water of the northern Kelly Bay, that together with the greater depth inside indicated that no glacier had its outlet in its bottom for a long time. In the inner part of this bay, two narrow, sack-like, rather small bays debouched, looking like estuaries. We had reconnoitred the northern bay at a previous time and had found it fairly short and without any major inflow of running water. It quickly lost itself in the marshlands in the interior of the valley. Therefore, we now steered for the southern bay. In this bay, a water-rich stream or river had its estuary, into which we advanced as far as possible in the increasing evening darkness. The stream became more and more filled with dead trees, standing upright in the water, and consequently we had soon to retreat downstream to be able to land and get a campsite. We landed finally on the north shore at a small lagoon-like expansion of the river, where we put up our tents in the pouring rain. However, the rain stopped eventually and was followed by a ghostly moonlight, which threw its brittle rays over the prehistoric, water glistening cypress landscape.

A campsite on the way to the Kelly Glacier

More dead trees on the way to the Kelly Glacier[03]

This cypress wood differed completely from the regular rain forest and was easy to pass. It stretched, grouped in groves, only a short distance away from the camp. After that wide, wobbling mirelands took over, where the depth to the solid sand ground was between one and two metres. Through the swampy landscape went zones of dead tree trunks, marking old water furrows. Here and there appeared larger fields of forest, where the unpleasant beech again made itself wide with its army of entangled and backbreaking companions. On these wide mires opened at last an opportunity to get a base long enough for the making of a map over the landscape. A lot of the time was also spent on this important job. In the inner part of the fjord, you saw the crevasse broken ice ridge of the Kelly Glacier at a distance. Behind this, the mountain ridges of the Cordilleras rose gradually up to the brilliant white and notchy watershed with the highest peaks of the chain of the Arenales to the south-east.

Swampy landscape

Wobbly mirelands[04]

Whoever transcends the edge of this watershed has then before himself the whole of Argentina, which rapidly absorbs the mountains and then passes into a low meseta landscape. Right in the transition between mountainous land and lowland there lies the 170-km-long Lago Buenos Aires [Lago General Carrera], mainly in Chilean, some in Argentine territory. The lake's altitude was only 277 metres above the sea and its distance as the crow flies was about 75 km from the point where we were standing. We had here in an east north-eastern direction one of the lower passes through the Cordilleras with a height of no more than 2000 metres between the 3440-metre-high Cerro San Valentin in the north and the equally high Cerro Arenales in the south. Without an auxiliary expedition on the Argentinian side, we could not think of crossing this desolate, wild and haunted area due to the nasty climate.

More wobbly mirelands

'Bush bashing' with axe on the way to the Kelly Glacier[05]

The solution to our task was to advance all the way to the ice of the Kelly Glacier using the first possible opportunity for this purpose. In this area we were able to advance comparatively quickly and somewhat straight, although we had to break through several troublesome forest strips, of course, under heavy rain. On cut-down tree trunks, we passed over a deep and broad stream, which carried some ten thousand litres of water per second. After finally having passed an extremely tangled, forested moraine ridge in the inner valley[05], we were standing in front of the glacier's fine-gravelled foreland. We were, however, still parted from that by a wide and shallow pool of water, ending against the edge of the moraine. After a couple of terrible rain showers had passed over the bleak landscape, we placed some fallen trees on the water. These could float us over to the about one-km-long, lovely gravel plain, where clusters of sedge and grass here and there were sticking up their shaving-brush-like tufts. Geese flew in huge flocks across the plain, screaming. A light rain kept on falling, and black clouds rolled over the mountain peaks. We therefore immediately divided ourselves into three groups to reconnoitre the terrain as quickly as possible. Nordenskjöld and Pedro went off towards the north edge of the glacier to advance along this and get an overview of the landscape itself. I got as my task, with Livorio, to seek the glacier tongue in the south to examine its drain through the side valley there. Rosen went with the gun in hand to enrich the zoological science as well as our own poorly supplied larder.

When we later met at the starting point, Nordenskjöld had managed to obtain detailed knowledge regarding the glacier's character and icing type and the geology of the area, together with the main features of its detailed topography in north direction[07]. I had penetrated the glacier's drainage valley, low, water

First view of the Kelly Glacier close up[06]

rich, wide, strangely shaped and further down between gloomy
forested hills strongly contracted. I completed this part of the
map. The glacier's tongue was at the outlet point at an altitude of 20 metres above sea level. Rosen returned to the meeting place with a juicy goose banging on his back[08]. After a wet
forced march, we returned to the camp, where we crawled all
wet into the sleeping bags. We smoked a comforting pipe and
devoured a cognac, before sleep again closed our eyes after one
of these typical Patagonian weekdays, when the life account
shows up in repulsive poverty. As we had turned off the lamp,
the tent was lit a couple of times by lightning, and the thunder
growled like a mountain troll over stolen secrets.

The outwash zone

Another advance was made to the glacier to complete the observations of the first excursion. Several side trips were also made to other places in the neighbourhood. Since thereafter the map had been complete, the earliest possible return to the camp was necessary before the tide had dropped so much that our return trip would be obstructed. After having loaded the boat we set off again, through the dead forests that rose from the bottom of the river. These dead trees are among the most enigmatic problems of the area. They consisted mainly of beech (*Quoihue*[09]) and cypress (*Libocedrus*[10]) and were partly strongly rotten. If you state the grade of rottenness on a 10-point scale, where zero represents full fresh wood and ten represents complete decay, the beech trunks were about 7. The cypresses were somewhat better preserved. Those standing dead tree trunks in the water must imply, that the watercourse had cut itself this new way fairly recently, perhaps very recently. Sometime later it had taken a different path again. Probably it had earlier used one or some of the overgrown furrows that we previously observed out in the marshes, and in these furrows perhaps had its outlets through the northern small bay.

Kelly Glacier

Kelly Glacier looking to the north

Kelly Glacier looking to the east[11]

Kelly Glacier, the west side

Kelly Glacier outwash

Kelly Glacier west side[12]

Kelly Glacier up by the ice

After returning to the coastal camp our work was mainly finished, as far as it could be completed by the Kelly Fjord. Only the details remained now to supplement it, as far as time and opportunity allowed. This occupied our time during those coming days, while waiting for the government steamer. The detailed task that especially attracted us was a survey of the southern shore area of the fjord, especially the so-called 'South Glacier'. This descended into a bay on the land between the Kelly Fjord and the Jesuitas Fjord, situated south of that. To get into the bay directly from our campsite was not possible because of the hindering sandbanks. The only way that seemed passable was to search your way from the mouth of the fjord, and into the southern outlet canal from the glacier. This branch flowed between one of the Boscosa's Islands and the southern shore of the fjord, as we have been able to clearly observe during ebb time from our elevated viewing points in the mountains above the coast camp.

Nordenskjöld and I, together with two of the Chilotes, made a rowing trip out there, but only to observe this rapidly flowing river branch. It was about 250 metres wide and carried enormous amounts of water - I calculated it to be approximately between 1,500 and 2,000 cubic metres per second. It was certainly completely free from everything that could be called sandbanks. It was instead breaking so heavily against the swell at its mouth, that as few as we were, we could not take our rather heavy boat up the river. From this glacier valley, into which also the Kelly Glacier's water was discharged, at least 6,000 cubic metres per second flowed out into the sea, and probably fairly uniformly over the year. This is about as much as the Danube, but from a catchment area which is just a few thousandths [of the size] of the Danube's. Nothing could lend itself better to giving a clear picture of the really enormous rainfall in these areas. Of course, this strong outflow is also largely due to the extremely low evaporation and infiltration.

On the way to survey the southern shore with the South Glacier (Glacier Benito)[13]

We landed in violent rain on the south side of the fjord, just off the river mouth and had to hurry to put up our tents on the sandy beach plain. The Chilotes, who for such trips had to their disposal a tent for two, never put up their tent the usual way. They placed it as an inclined screen, leaning on some sloping tree trunks. Inside they then made the fire and were lying protected from the rain and got on rather well. The approach had a striking resemblance to the tenting methods of the Patagonian Indians.

The campsite next to the beach. Note the Chilotes' lean to tent

We stayed here overnight. But it was to be a troubled night because the boat, our only hope, was about to tear away from its inadequate moorings on the low beach side and make off to the sea. I was woken up around two o'clock in the night by the terribly roaring tide, which was rapidly approaching the tent. 'The boat!' I thought, and jumped up, threw on my boots and rushed out in the dark, in which the phosphorescent surf was shining like the froth around a fool's lips. The boat had nearly keeled over in the waves, and the oars had just started to float away. In the last moment I got a hold on them by running far out in the water and pulled them back on the beach. I then secured the boat where it was, as good as I could in the darkness, and woke up the Chilotes. With their help the boat was hauled far up on the beach, a fire was lit and guard posted until the tide again began to fall and morning dawned for a new and beautiful day.

The boat with the Professor on the beach

The camp was delightfully located on the edge of the forest, which was descending down a steep hill with ferns, fuchsias and lianas in a richness and splendour reminding us of Italy. On the beach was not a crab, not a star fish, not a living being seen, probably depending on the brackish water from the nearby glacial river. Out in the Gulf of San Quintin, the surf threw its sunlit, proud white plumes high towards heaven, like a ringing call from distant beaches. This calm day with its drowsy endless swell, its blue skies reminding of our immortal souls, and the far away marching rain flurries, instilled peace and happiness for the soul. It awoke hundreds of beautiful memories to life, these treasures, of which no one can deprive us.

After breakfast, we advanced upwards along the banks of the glacier river as far as we could. After the place had been plundered of observations, we got into the boat and followed the coastline outwards and further on into the little fjord on the side, aiming south. Seals were playing around rock islands in the mouth of the fjord. Mighty marine algae (*Macrocystis*) grew by the foots of the beach rocks and were exposed now and then. The unfathomable forces of the ocean slowly lifted and lowered the surface of the sea to the bottom and laid bare this passive world. It was a real Sunday row over the serene fjord, one of these bright moments, that made the dark ones seven times worse, but also heightened the moments and us to a life fit for human beings.

Allan Bäckman with a mossy branch – view up Kelly Inlet

It was now 1ˢᵗ February, but no ship had yet been seen. The supplies were scarce and had become scarcer than expected, because some had been destroyed by the climate. Some had unfortunately not followed us ashore. If anything should happen to the expected steamer, our position would be very critical. Admittedly, we had rifles and ammunition with us to hunt and replenish our supplies, but wildlife in the Kelly Fjord was insignificant both in terms of species and in numbers. On the coast there are no geese or other birds suitable for food. A white heron had occasionally trimmed its beautiful plumage, outside gunshot distance on the sandbanks in the fjord outside our camp. Sometimes you might see some hummingbird, unmovable in the air, hovering on wings swift as an arrow in front of a pink flower bell, trembling from passion over this moment of infinity. Sometimes you could see albatrosses on motionless wings inspect the fjord. Once we had seen a flock of green parrots in the vicinity of the coast camp, and from there we could sometimes hear the yells of the bird, that further up in Chile is called *vanduria*[14]. Their short and sharp trumpet calls are confusingly reminiscent of the sound of a modern car horn. Our company and our intimate friends were the grebes, who were also the most characteristic creatures in the Kelly Fjord. They came daily, swimming with the tide and with their curved beaks lifted in the air and the long necks swinging in pace with the strokes, and at ebb time again moved outwards against the mouth of the fjord. We never saw them fly. In contrast they dived with great skill, after having passed us so close, that their fear now exceeded their obvious curiosity. In fair weather you could hear their calls incessantly, in foul weather more seldom. Often, they called late at night or very early in the morning. The sound was not unlike a meowing kitten, especially from a distance. They never came within gunshot and therefore never ended up in our stew.

Grebes in Kelly Fjord

But when hunting, while waiting for the boat, became an imperative necessity, we had to seek the prey that was missing in our neighbourhood. It was then to the estuary of the fjord that we wended our way. Hunting trips there were undertaken alternately by all the expedition members, but it was essentially the zoologist Rosen who had to hunt, and he undertook this task in a great way. For a start he shot cormorants, on which we cooked an excellent *cazuela* (Chilean national dish, cooked meat, grains and potatoes, etc). But the birds soon enough got timid and unapproachable, and to our distress and anxiety finally disappeared from the neighbourhood. The rations were then halved, and we all went with a constant hunger in the pit of the stomach. We even had to try the lean and bland soup that the Chilotes cooked on the sea algae, a weak dish, that only made the feeling of hunger so much more pinching. The pleasure was therefore great when Nordenskjöld and Rosen after a brilliant hunting trip came back to our port with two seals. These mighty beasts filled for a long time our food supply. After intensive boiling this meat offered a powerful dish, which could however reasonably be said to be more tough than good. But all eagerly ate all that was offered. To put a little gilt edge to the herculean chewing work, the remaining aquavit supply was rationed, and dispensed every other day with five centilitres measured in a graduated glass. If you kept on with this camp life for a longer time, this would probably end up as second nature.

Drying food (Kelp) at Base Camp

A beautiful morning – i.e. moderately beautiful - I said to Nordenskjöld with whom I shared one of the Chilote tents, 'Now I feel that the boat is soon coming'. Ten minutes later, Bäckman's call was heard from his thermometers' cage, 'The boat is coming!' It was 9th February. The joy was great, not least among the Chilotes, who for a couple of weeks daily had gazed out to the sea.

It was again the old *Yañez* out there in the fjord to retrieve us. Its sympathetic commander Captain Merino arrived ashore immediately after the anchoring, with his two ship's boats to hasten the departure in the calm weather.

The Captain with one of his flock!

In three hours, the camp was broken with luggage and collections carried onboard in the boat. Without delay we lifted anchor and went out into the Golfo de Penas. The haste with which we got torn away from our environment was almost brutal. With a strange mixture of joy and sadness, we saw the Kelly Fjord, the San Tadeo Glacier and San Javier sink below the line of sight in the east, over the peaky waves of the gulf.

Our return journey was made at a record speed. It took close
to a hundred hours, although we had to stay in Puerto Barroso
in the western part of the Golfo de Penas the first 24 hours
because of bad weather. We enjoyed ourselves with mollusc
fishing, which was extremely rich in this old whale hunting
station. Then the journey continued across the Pacific Ocean,
which this time was sunny and calm and only gracefully lifted
us on its wandering waves. We followed the coast over Ana
Pink Bay all the way up to Analao. The big island Huamblin[15]
raised its peaks up from the sea and the last outpost of the
Chonos Archipelago, Ypun with Cape Lort disappeared in the
blue mist of the distance. From there, we steered directly into
the Darwin Canal and stayed overnight in Puerto Yates inside
the Garrido Island.

In the cabin of the Yañez – *from the left Nils, Allan, Prof and Sten*

Early the following morning we proceeded directly to Puerto
Montt. After a cloudy trip through the channels, we arrived
there on the evening of 13th February 1921. In the morning of

the same day, we had parted from our loyal Chilotes in Queilén on Chiloé. They left the ship on our old longboat *Eriksson*, which they received as a well-deserved gift. It was with regret we saw them shove off from the *Yañez* and disappear in the grey morning, and the regret was apparently mutual.

Livorio, Pedro and Olegari leaving Yañez *in the longboat*

Extracts from Allan Bäckman's Letters

Allan remained at Base Camp whilst the Professor, Nils Pallin, Sten von Rosen and two Chilotes explored Kelly Glacier (now Glacier Andree).

Allan at his meteorological station

Thursday, 27th January 1921. On January 26th, the others returned home from their trip to the Kelly Glacier. It became so noisy and distracting, so I could not write anything. It was decided that Rosen the next day, i.e. today, would go with the boat and two Chilotes out to the fjord estuary we crossed in for zoological collections. When I did not have anything for me, I decided to go and this morning we started at a quarter past six from here. Of course, it rained, but it cleared at 7 o'clock and then we had beautiful weather all day.

It was a wonderful trip! It was completely windless, the sun was shining so wonderfully nice, it was really like a spring day at home. I made small map sketches of the fjord shores, took photographs in abundance and by the way helped Rosen when he needed a pair of strong arms. We came all the way out to the northern cape (Punta Blanca), then crossed the fjord and followed that shore to the east. At 12 o'clock we entered a small fjord bay, which was still unknown. In front of the mouth of the fjord pocket were a few islands, which I quietly named 'January 27 Islands'. There we landed for cooking and were lucky enough to get into the middle of a bird colony, with nests and not fully fledged chicks.

With the rifle, we shot several older and younger specimens and rejoiced at the thought of the wonderful 'casuela' (Spanish stew), which would be eaten tomorrow. There on the island I also picked a little flower! But soon it clouded over again and threatened with rain, so we decided to return. On the way home

Two of the Chilotes at the water's edge

no less than two seals were shot, but we did not recover either of them. A dead seal always sinks, and here the water was so deep that we did not catch them properly. But the pride did not decrease, on the contrary it rose! At 4 pm we were back in the camp and now we have coffee. I have lit the pipe and produced this book.

Tomorrow, Prof and Pallin intend to set off for the 'southern glacier' (aka Glacier Benito). I have said that they will never succeed in reaching it. It's going to be fun to see if I'm right. But the sleeping bag attracts so wonderfully, and I am cold about the midriff!

Wednesday, 2nd February 1921. Today we write as I said on 2nd February and the boat has not arrived yet. Incidentally, this is not so strange, because the weather of the last few days has made all sea voyages impossible. Firstly, it has blown a misty north wind and secondly, the perpetual rain and fog has made it impossible to navigate in these virtually unknown waters. Therefore, the boat is probably waiting for better weather somewhere in a sheltered harbor in the Peninsular de Taitao direction. One can certainly not imagine how intense it rained yesterday, but one can possibly get a faint idea of it, if I say that yesterday between 8 in the morning and 7:30 in the evening fell as much rain as during two months in Stockholm. If we count, as usual, the night's precipitation to the previous day's, we get a figure which is 1/5 of the entire annual precipitation in the beautiful Mälardrottningen! If you are thinking of a gale from the north, then you probably understand why people do not like to stick their noses out of the tent.

I lay in the sleeping bag almost all day, leaving its pleasant warmth only at the observations and meals. At 3 am last night I woke up to the 'angriest' rain shower (hail mixed)

I have ever heard, turned on the light, squinted and looked at the barometer. It had fallen to 738.3 mm (984 mbar), a pretty respectable figure. But soon after that the rain stopped, the barometer began an insane dance upwards, and the wind turned west and southwest. Now (at 9:30 in the morning) the weather is fair, but the wind is fresh. And it's a question of whether the boat dares cross the Golfo de Penas in this wind. There is a little more movement in the camp today. As usual, Prof is repackaging then unpacking his rags and small packages. Pallin is busy with basic measurement. Rosen has stepped out into the woods to collect mosquitoes. I am sitting here writing! Once Pallin has got the base and stations in order, I will set up the theodolite and take some angles, but until then I will take care of nothing but my (meteorological) observations.

Sunday, 6ᵗʰ February 1921. Yesterday was one of the most beautiful days we have so far enjoyed in Estera Chacualat (I have certainly always written Chacaulat, but that is wrong!). It was high, clean air, quite warm and - sunshine.

We have not had an abundance of it! There was also an energetic photo shoot in the camp, which made all of us say 'unprintable words'. Here you photograph the same thing on a lot of plates, necessary because the prospect of the plates being damaged by the constant moisture is extremely great. I noticed it with concern last night, when I put new plates in the cassettes. The gelatine membranes become soft, stick to each other and the whole thing is destroyed. Therefore, I always take double photos of objects of greater value, i.e. I take a photo on sheet metal and one on flat film. The latter seems to do better in this climate. My camera is excellent. The others all have 2 pcs. cameras each. But in any case, no one competes with mine. Except of course Rosen's SLR camera, but it's a completely different type, and since it does not have a tripod, it cannot compete with mine anyway.

The expedition team in 1920 in Patagonia[16] from left to right Nils Pallin, Allan Bäckman, Professor Otto Nordenskjöld and Sten von Rosen

Yesterday was thus photo day. In vain we scouted for the boat in the evening and therefore it was decided during the war council after supper, that Prof and Rosen was going on a three to four day hunting trip out in the fjord estuary. The last time Rosen got eight cormorants, which was enough for 2½ 'casuela' (Spanish stew). Today (the 6th) they also left, and Pallin and I were alone in the camp with a Chilote. But why is the boat delayed? The last few days the weather has been the best possible. Have they perhaps forgotten us? It is not so conceivable as Prof, in addition to the written submission to the authorities, also notified Capt. Krook and the Swedish consul Heavy that we must be picked up around the 1st of February because our stores do not last longer than the 10th. Or has there been a revolution in Chile? Then at least Krook and the consul would take matters into their own hands and make sure we were picked up.

Allan, Prof and Nils in front of a tent

Or has there been an earthquake and everyone who knows we are here is dead? Well, it's not worth thinking about. If the boat arrives before the 15ᵗʰ, everything is fine, because until then we can manage with food. But if it does not come by then, well, then the tragic part of the story begins. It is doubtful whether we will get away from it all with life. But as I said, the day will come, the help will come. Now I have to go out in the sunshine for a while!

Wednesday, 9ᵗʰ February 1921. At 8:10 am. Two minutes ago, we discovered the boat! Hip, hip, hooray!

Thursday, 10ᵗʰ February 1921, Port Otway. On the 6ᵗʰ I last wrote. As I said, Prof and Rosen went on a hunting trip. They headed for the 'January 27 Islands' and left Pallin and me alone in the camp. I then wrote a few lines, strutted around for a while in the sunshine, and when it started to rain shortly afterwards I withdrew to the tent and cooked. The day went by and the night surprised with a glorious storm, rain and wind. 7ᵗʰ February was similar with bad

weather as well. It rained with small breaks between showers. Towards noon we saw the little boat coming. I went
into the tent to start making coffee. Meanwhile the boat
landed and I heard surprised exclamations from Pallin and
happy triumphant ditto from Prof and Rosen. The reason
was two large seals, which had to give their lives to increase
our food supply. The innermost of the 'January 27 Islands'
had turned out to be a seal colony and with two shots
Rosen had shot two magnificent animals. It eased the wor-
ries somewhat. Seal meat is disgusting, but when it comes
to not starving, it probably tastes heavenly. So now we had
meat for several days ahead, and knew the place where we
could get more.

Returning with dead seals

The mood rose several degrees, somewhat facilitated by
schnapps and a bottle of champagne for dinner.

A tent at Camp 1 with Sten von Rosen

The 8th started as usual with the morning coffee served by me. The 'old man' starts off frying seal meat, salts the rest or takes care of it in another way. But damn it! Seal meat is awful. It was served with boiled potatoes as lunch on the 8th. I ate very little of it. The only one who seemed to value it was Prof[17]. He certainly did not like it either. However, he was too stingy not to eat, when he got the food for free, so to speak. With the help of pepper, vinegar and mustard one tried to make it more enjoyable, that decision was unanimous. So, the day went on. The Chilotes were busy preparing sealskins. We strutted around and photographed and looked in vain for *Yañez*.

Then it was seen on the 9th Wednesday.

As usual, I was up at 8 o'clock for observation, made my morning coffee and sunbathed for a while. Rosen and I discussed the preparations for the steak roast. When we agreed on the recipe, I took the knife and stripped out pieces of meat, which hung on an oar. Right next to me is a Chilote looking out to the mouth of the fjord. Suddenly he says in his calm way: 'Ya está el vapor! Ya viene! ' (Spanish 'The steamboat is already here. It's coming.') It hit me. I jumped down to the thermometer cage to get a good view. Really! Out there in the gap, the contours of a small steamboat were seen heading into Kelly Inlet. No doubt possible! I shouted loudly: 'The boat is here!' What a happy message the other expeditioners threw their heads out of their sleeping bags and tents. Soon we were all overjoyed and watched as the boat dropped anchor just west of the western waterfall valley.

So, a quick breakfast was started, canned food and great coffee. Prof, Pallin and Rosen got ready to go on board and I stopped to cook a stately farewell dinner, to which the boat's Captain would be invited. I had only baked one pudding (vanilla!) when the others returned, together with our Captain from the first trip. But dinner went awry.

Loading the boats in Kelly Inlet ready for the voyage home

The Captain was in a great hurry. In three hours, we must be ready and cross the Golfo de Penas in the beautiful weather. Said and done. At 12 we definitely left our station and at 1 pm *Yañez* started the propeller. When we came out on the Golfo de Penas and had a view of the whole area, where we worked and toiled for seven weeks. The sun pushed away the cloud cover and there the snow-covered mountains and glaciers lay sparkling in the sunlight. It was stately, unforgettable sight! Goodbye, Kelly! And so, we headed out to the Golfo de Penas. The wind was weak north-east, but the swell came strong and powerful from the south-west and, of course, made me seasick. But it didn't bother me at all, I'm on my way home! Then everything is fine!

All aboard on the way back – Captain, Prof, Allan and Sten

Tuesday, 15th February 1921, Puerto Montt! At dawn on the 13th, we were therefore outside Queilén, where we were to hand over our three Chilotes. They were paid, got a little extra money and also everything we did not think worthwhile transporting

home. Their countenance shone with delight for every little trifle, for every shard that was bestowed upon them. But they had
also honestly deserved everything. They were willing and helpful, did not budge, were happy and content in the most devilish
conditions. Pedro and Liborio in particular were magnificent
individuals. Oligari loafed sometimes, but if you watched him
carefully he would assist, too.

My contributions to the gifts consisted of the American
boots and the raincoat. The former went to Pedro, the latter
to Liborio. Both would be irreparable. The sharpest micro-
scope could not have shown the slightest hint of either soles or
heels. In the toe of the right shoe gaped a large hole that had
arisen when I cut the tent pole in the glacier camp. The axe
had slanted, of course, and went in through the shoe but was
stopped by the toe cap before it had time to scratch more than
the big toe. The raincoat had no less than seven large holes.
All had been battered during the climb in Patagonia's primeval
forests. I was probably thinking of saving it, but when I saw
Liborio's radiant face and felt his grateful handshake when he
received it, I did not regret my waste.

On the other hand, I weep bitterly over the loss of Jonte's
leather vest! It was completely permeated during my memora-
ble hike over the mountains. I first tried to dry it in the tent, but
when it did not work, I had to hang it next to the campfire and
it could not stand it. The skin shrunk, partially cracked by itself
and still cracked more when I tried to pull it on me. Since not
even the Chilotes wanted it, I did not consider it worth taking
home. It is now at the camp site in Chacualat in the company
of a pair of my leg wraps, a pair of thin underwear and my old-
est braces. I had used the underwear during the entire Peru trip
and half the stay in Patagonia and was full of holes! I have used
the leg wraps all the time. They looked like nothing! That's all

that was definitely lost to me during this expedition. The rest is so far intact, although more or less destroyed by moisture and abrasion. However, it can be repaired and used. Unless it's stolen from me on the way home.

Livorio, Pedro and Olegari heading for shore in the longboat

✧

Chapter 7

NILS PALLIN'S MAP, NOTES AND AFTERWORD

The Map [AJ]

Nils Pallin published the map below with his article in the *Alpine Journal* titled 'Mountains And Glaciers In West Patagonia', published in No. 45, 1933.

Nils Pallin's Notes

1) About this Daniel Forelius, Captain Gösta Krook in Valparaiso found information that partly formed the basis of a brief but captivating biography. It was written by Carl Forsstrand after further research and included in his book "Svenska lyckoriddare i främmande länder" (Hugo Gebers förlag, Stockholm, 1916). For some reason Forelius's name has not been included in the book's table of contents. Forelius was born in 1787 and the son of the rural court judge, Carl Forelius. After completing university studies, he entered the legal profession and made an official career, advancing to be a court of review secretary in 1818. After an unusually beautiful career, he suddenly requested and was granted a 'graceful' retirement in 1821 and went to Chile, where he won military employment and as secretary

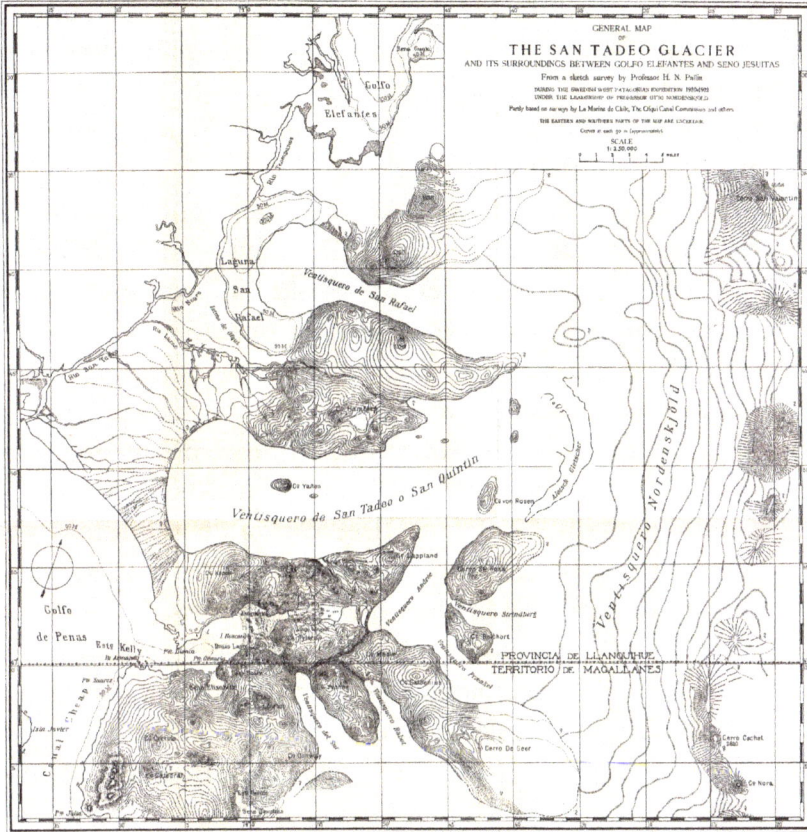

Mountains and glaciers in West Patagonia [AJ]

to the governor of Chiloé. There he became acquainted with Fitz-Roy, the reputable commander of the navy brig *Beagle,* famous through Darwin's world tour. During his maritime survey of the Patagonian coast, Fitz-Roy, apparently from high esteem of the excellent Swede, fixed his name on the large peninsula. Forelius later got involved in politics and participated in the revolution against the dictator Prieto, but was captured along with several other participants in the revolt and was shot at Plaza Victoria in

Valparaiso on July 4, 1837. In Sweden he had been united
with the sculptor Sergel's only daughter in a childless mar-
riage, and in Chile he left a native wife. Several descendants of his belong to the prominent Valparaiso families
Bianchi and Rivera Blin.

2) See Charles Darwin: "Resa kring jorden", publisher *Natur
   & kultur,* Stockholm, 1925 [i.e. The Voyage of the Beagle].
   In this classic, soon ninety years old and extremely interesting travel book, the renowned scientist leaves rich
   and overlapping descriptions of those parts, such as they
   appeared about a century ago[01].

3) Allan Bäckman has submitted to the proceedings of
   the 17th Scandinavian Natural Scientists Meeting in
   Gothenburg in 1923 [i.e. "Det sjuttonde skandinaviska
   naturforskaremötet i Göteborg, den 9-14 juli 1923"] "Två
   nya bidrag till Väst-Patagoniens klimatologi" [i.e. "Two
   new contributions to the climatology of West Patagonia"],
   to which the meteorologically interested reader is referred
   for details on this strange climate.

4) This is a problem for the specialists, although it cannot
   cease to fascinate us human beings also. I have been wondering about the same coal formation on Svalbard as well,
   asking myself how it is possible for such a rich coal flora
   to occur in a part of the Earth, where there is uninterrupted night for four to five months of the year. It is possible that the Arctic coal could support the theory of pole
   movements. It is also possible that the same coal can give
   an explanation of the origin of the mineral oil. Coal deposits, ignited by lightning in ancient times, can burn for
   centuries with low air supply and generate liquid hydro-
   carbons. These sink through the rock layers into holes and
   spaces in the lower areas of the earth crust, where they are

then slowly converted into petroleum. After this excursion to the theoretical and speculative hunting grounds of science, we may return to those of West Patagonia.

5) One occurrence that looks like more than a coincidence, is that Dr. F. Reichert started an expedition from Santiago to the same ice field immediately after us, also with the support of a Chilean government steamer. He landed with his men in Lago San Rafael, and advanced from here under the most disgusting weather conditions up the San Rafael Glacier, in the direction of Cerro San Valentin. On 11 January 1921, the weather finally admitted an overview of the landscape. He then made essentially the same observations as us. Though our general view from the summit of the 'Bowler', as well as what we observed in our investigations along the San Tadeo Glacier and its border mountains, must have been more extensive.

✧

Afterword

P rofessor Otto Nordenskjöld [02] continued with his Professorial role at the University of Gothenburg. He made a presentation on his expedition to South America to the Swedish Society for Anthropology and Geography on 18th November 1921. In 1923, Otto Nordenskjöld published a 240 page 'text' book titled *People and Nature in South America* in Swedish (*Människor och natur i Sydamerika*). Sadly he died in a traffic accident outside his house in Gothenburg on 2nd June 1928 when he was 59. In Chile he is remembered by Lago Nordenskjöld.

Professor Nordenskjöld

Nils Pallin[03] went on to have a very industrious career. He continued working at the Road and Water Management Board and in various districts until 1932 and was road consultant in Gotland County from 1924 to 1930. He was vice president of the Swedish Technology Association's Department of Road and Water Engineering 1924.

Nils qualified as a professor in road construction and communication technology at the Royal Institute of Technology in Stockholm in 1925, became deputy professor in 1929, ordinary professor from 1932 and departmental director since 1937. He attained the rank of lieutenant colonel in 1939.

After Nils retired from the Royal Institute of Technology, he accepted a position as professor of traffic technology at the University of Istanbul. He was tasked with the modernization of the curriculum and methods of the department. After three years in Turkey, he returned home in 1950.

Nils became a member of the Alpine Club in 1929, was one of the founders and first chairman of the Swedish Army Reserve Officers' Association in 1924 and one of the founders and first chairman of the Swedish Association of Writers in 1934.

Nils led geographic expeditions to Spitzbergen in 1922, 1923, and 1928, then to Iceland in 1935 and to Greenland in 1936. He discovered several new 2000-meter-high peaks in Lapland and in 1927-28 completed a cross-country skiing journey from Tromsø in northernmost Norway, along the mountain ridge forming the border between Norway and Sweden (called Kölen, i.e. The Keel) all the way to Oslo, about 2,000 km south.

In addition to the writings mentioned below, Nils compiled a Swedish mountain catalogue, *Svensk fjällkatalog* (1922), and published a new edition of P. Tillaeus's map of Stockholm dating from 1733 in 1925. He was editor of the periodical *Vägen* (The road) from 1936 and wrote numerous articles in trade journals and in the daily press using the signatures 'HNP' and 'Pan'.

The list of writings, post expedition, most of them in Swedish, include:

- 'Kebnekaise' (1927) (about trips and adventures in Lapland)
- 'Naturlagar för trafiken' (1928) (The natural laws of traffic)
- 'Trafikens världsherravälde' (1932) (World dominion of traffic)
- 'Mountains and Glaciers in West Patagonia' (in: *Alpine Journal*, 1933)
- *Andréegåtan* (1934) (The mystery of the Andrée tragedy)
- *Mountains and Glaciers in West Greenland* (1937)
- 'Vägarna och naturskyddet' (1937) (Roads and nature conservation and protection)
- 'Trafiken som samhällsomdanare' (1940) (Traffic as reorganizer of society)

Nils Pallin died in September 1953, aged 73.

Sten von Rosen[04]. In the Gothenburg Natural History Museum, there is material from Sten von Rosen that he collected on the expedition, registered in the catalogues and in the database. This includes four boxes with collections of insects and some mammals like paca, pacarana, seal, undetermined deer, brocket and mice. In the museum's archive there are documents related to him and the collected material, including his field catalogues, permits for transport, etc. Some letters exist between the museum's director, Professor L.A. Jägerskiöld, and Sten.

A couple of years after the expedition, Sten was asked to take part in Sven Hedin's expedition to central Asia, but had to reject the offer due to health difficulties. Later, he went on an expedition trip to Abyssinia (Ethiopia), where he visited Addis Ababa and the area south of it and was at the Emperor's (Haile Selassie) coronation in 1930. He also went to 'Främre orienten' (the Middle East) finding both ethnographic material and material connected to natural science. The trips were not good for his health since he became sick with typhus. His health problems due to typhus put obstacles in his plans to travel and there were no more expeditions. Instead he continued learning more about his old interest but also philosophy and social science.

Sten was a man that didn´t talk much of himself but he was loved by his friends and he sometimes invited them to his farm 'Kröngården' in the province Jämtland. He moved in October 1937 to Nizza (Nice) in France, where he died 16th March 1939 after an operation. He was buried on 27th March 1939 at Solna cemetery in Stockholm. His collections, mainly from Abyssinia, were donated to The Royal Swedish Academy of Sciences.

Sten von Rosen[05]

Allan Bäckman[06] published 'Västpatagonins klimatologi'[07] (West Patagonia Climatology) in 1922 and 'L´influence de l´altitude et de la position géographic sur la températur de láir dans la région sud-oust de la Suéd' (The influence of altitude and geographic position on the air temperature in the south-western region of Sweden) in 1927. In 1927, he became filosofie licentiat ('fil.lic.') which was a university degree equivalent to a PhD, obtained after two years further study after ordinary examination. After that he was the CEO of the company Edwin Thomeé AB in Malmö. He was the member of several boards in the Malmö area and in July 1939 was appointed to consul for Norway in Malmö. He married Elna Montgomery, and they had four children, Greta, Anna-Lisa, Tora and Kerstin. He died on 28th August 1956 in Malmö.

Allan Bäckman in later life[08]

On the way home to Sweden

Epilogue and the Changes
SUBSEQUENT EXPLORATION

At the same time that Professor Nordenskjöld and his expedition was investigating Glacier San Quintin from Kelly Inlet [Map of Routes of Glacier San Quintin and Kelly Inlet, route 1], Reichert[01] and his expedition came by ship down the inland route via Golfo de Elephantes to Laguna San Rafael [Map of Routes of Glacier San Quintin and Kelly Inlet, route 2]. They went to the south side of the Laguna to the old crossing point of the Istmo de Ofqui, before ascending Glacier San Rafael along the north valley side. They reached the Nunatak before returning to the Laguna.

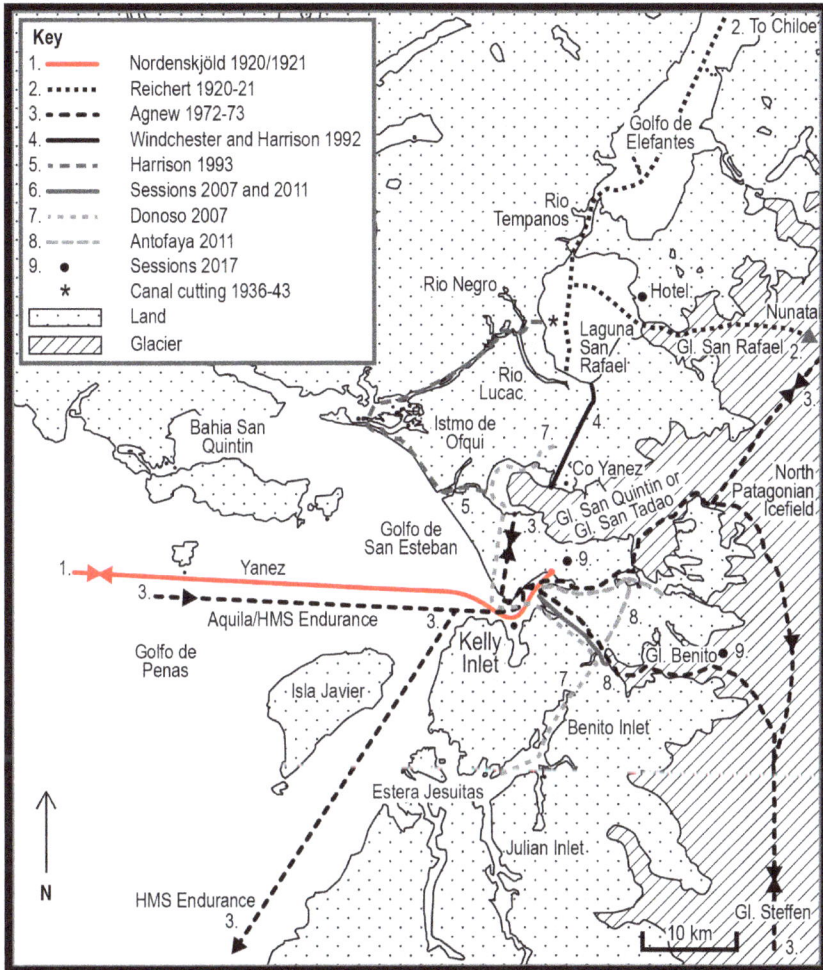

Map of routes to Glacier San Quintin and Kelly Inlet after 1921

More survey work was undertaken by the Istmo de Ofqui Canal Commission in the 1930s in Laguna San Rafael area. This culminated in commencement of digging the canal between the Laguna and Rio Negro between 1937 and 1943 when funds ran out[02]. A hotel was built on the north side of Laguna San Rafael which opened for just one night in 1938!

The next significant event was in 1944 when the entire ice-field was overflown and photographed from 18,000 feet by the United States Air Force. The system used was the Trimetrogon aerial camera system which consisted of a vertical camera and two cameras pointing out, one to each side mounted in the air-craft. Over the next 20 years, maps were generated, albeit not very accurate with respect to contours as there was no ground control. Nevertheless, this contributed to several expeditions climbing a number of peaks. Monte San Valentin, the highest mountain on the icefield, was first climbed in 1952 and Cerro Arenales, the second highest, in 1958.

Although Kelly Inlet may have had periodic visitors since 1921, these would have been fishermen and sailing ships. As Kelly Inlet was off the beaten track, these visits must have been very few.

The longest occupation of Kelly Inlet occurred in the austral summer of 1972/73 by the British Joint Services Expedition to Chilean Patagonia led by Crispin Agnew[03]. This expedi-tion was inspired by the explorer Eric Shipton's book *Land of Tempest* and his 1964 crossing of the North Patagonian Icefield from Glacier San Rafael to Glacier Arenales[04]. The expedition required a site that was readily accessible by the Royal Navy's Antarctic ice patrol ship, HMS *Endurance,* which brought the bulk of the supplies and equipment and provided valuable support with its two Whirlwind helicopters. Kelly Inlet was the logical choice for the starting point of the expedition.

The expedition team arrived on the Chilean Navy ship, *Aquilla,* on 31st October 1972 and set up base camp to the west of the Professor's base camp. HMS *Endurance* arrived on 7th December to lift a large quantity of stores to the icefield for the assault on Monte San Valentin. In late December and early January, the eleven-man team crossed the ice field to the mountain but were unable to climb it due to the high avalanche risk resulting from much fresh snow in January 1973.

Over the five months, the expedition team undertook numerous studies and measurements on Glacier Benito, fixed several survey points, undertook a comprehensive hydrographic survey of Kelly Inlet, trekked to the terminus of Glacier Steffen in the south, maintained a meteorological station and made many other studies [Map of Routes of Glacier San Quintin and Kelly Inlet, route 3]. The Professor's route to Glacier Andrée was used many times as the expedition crossed this glacier from the west side to the east side to get to the advanced

JSE Chilean Patagonia 1972/73. Left to right standing – Jonathan, Peter, Chris, Crispin, Angus, Teuch, Stuart, Bill and Neil. Kneeling – Martin and John

base camp high up on Glacier San Quintin. After nearly five months the expedition was picked up in foul weather by HMS *Endurance* on 20th March 1973.

A summary of the expedition appeared in the Geographical Magazine[05] and is reproduced here with the permission of its author, Crispin Agnew.

Map-making on the Patagonian ice-cap

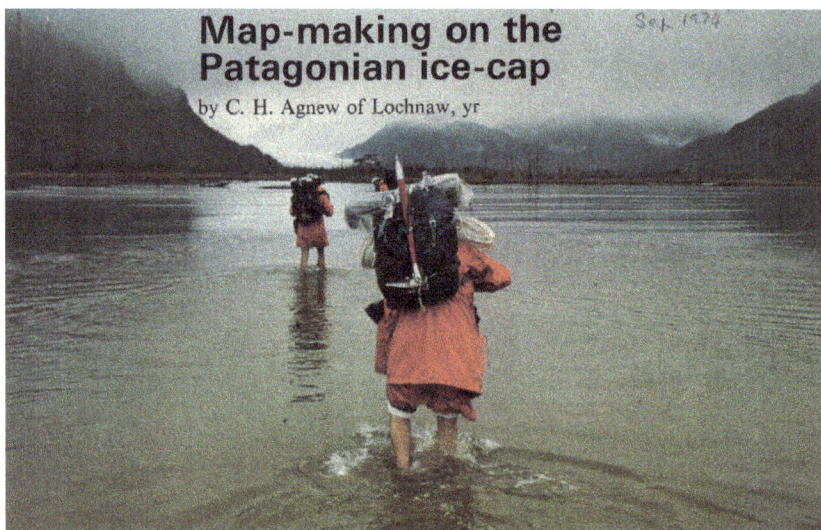

Map-making on the Patagonian ice-cap
by C. H. Agnew of Lochnaw, yr

Dense rain forest bars the route to Chile's northern ice-cap,
the Hielo Patagonia del Norte. It presented a severe obstacle to
a British Joint Services expedition which set out to survey the area. (Above)
Wading ashore at the head of Kelly Inlet through the icy glacial meltwater.

THE HIELO PATAGONIA DEL NORTE, Chile's northern ice-cap, lies at 47° south, or the same latitude as Switzerland is north, and 73° west. But here the similarity ends. The coast is fjorded and the steep slopes are heavily forested to 600 metres with an almost impenetrable temperate rain forest which reaches right down to the high tide line, where the roots are exposed by the waves. Behind this guard of trees lie the glaciers and ice-cap. The glaciers, which push into the forest are fast flowing and heavily crevassed with great ridges and pinnacles peculiar to Patagonia. The ice-cap has relatively easy terrain but is beset by some of the worst weather in the world. The area lies in the southern depression belt, on the fringes of the roaring forties. With the moisture from the forests, heavy rain, strong wind and almost continuous cloud cover on the ice-cap makes travel and navigation particularly difficult.

Landing in Kelly Inlet

On a dismal October evening, the Joint Services Expedition 1972-1973 was landed by the Chilean warship *Aquilla* on the beach of the Kelly Inlet at low tide in the rain. The party of eleven drawn from the three services had been flown to Puerto Montt in southern Chile, in a Royal Air Force Hercules and then carried south by the Chilean Navy. Before the next high tide, we had to make a clearing in the forest for our fifteen tons of stores, move them off the beach and pitch tents uncomfortably for the first night. We were here for five months to try to make the first survey of the area from which to produce a corrected and revised edition of the local Carta Preliminar, which was drawn from uncontrolled air photography taken in 1943. In addition, we were to make a geological survey, a study of the glaciology of the Benito Glacier and undertake other scientific tasks.

After we had cleared the forest for base camp, built our small hut and settled in, we started on the survey. Captain Jon Zorijack, a surveyor from the Royal Engineers, who was coordinating this work, established the first triangulation station on Punta Blanca, a sand spit, siting the mark on some rocks. He settled down with theodolite, chronometer, a radio for the time checks and star tables to await a break in the permanent cloud cover. It was essential to establish the geographical position of the first station by astronomical fixing as a starting point to the traverse. We planned to carry the traverse through a series of stations up on to the ice-cap, south for thirty-two kilometres, down the Benito Glacier and then finish at the inlet station. Jon Zorijack, helped by Lieutenant Chris Gobey, a Royal Naval Hydrographer, spent almost the whole of November trying to get sufficient star sights to fix the position to third order standard. Cloud cover was the main problem as even on good nights at least half the sky was obscured. When the position was finally calculated, it appeared that the given longitude was three seconds (or nautical miles) in error to the west.

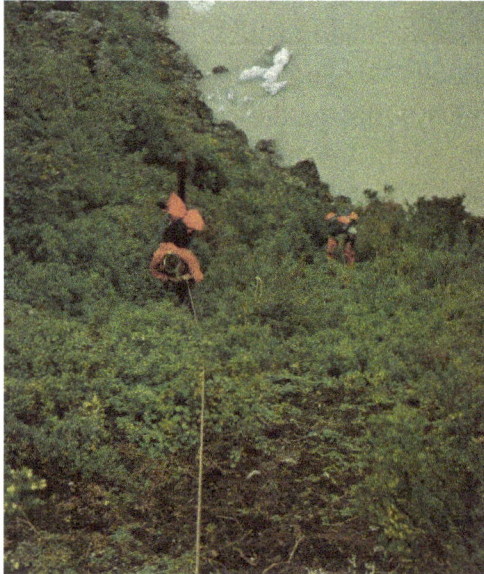

Forest gave way to scrub on the way to the ice-cap

Route through the forest to Andrée Glacier had later to be followed by surveyors with heavy equipment. (Above) Camp at the snout of the glacier. To the south a range of mountains divides the ice-cap into two - beyond them the Steffen Glacier flows southwards. Route led up the Andrée Glacier to the icecap.

While the surveyors were in siege on the first survey station, l had to find a route to the ice-cap up the Andrée Glacier, selecting and checking possible survey stations for intervisibility. In all I spent fifteen days trying to force a route ten miles up to the ice-cap. First we had to go through five kilometres of forest, which was reached by boat up the Kelly Inlet from base camp. It took five hours to push a route through the forest. The tangle of fallen trees, creepers, holly bushes and moss made it very unpleasant work. lt was clearly impracticable to carry the heavy loads of a survey station through it, so three members of the expedition spent seven days clearing a path through the forest of the Andrée Glacier cutting the journey from the inlet to the glacier to three hours.

From a level section between ice-falls,
Mount San Valentin could be seen on clear days

Meantime I continued with two other members of the party, trying to find a practical route up the Andrée Glacier. My first attempt ended in a complex ice-fall after two hours. The next, a six-day trip, took two days to reach the glacier via a short cut through the forest, then a day to cross its 2-mile width through a complicated crevasse system. The Patagonian glaciers are like no other because, where crevasses open, the sides ablate away leaving narrow ridges instead of flat areas between the cracks. These knife-edged ridges have cross-crevasses, which make them into pinnacles. By the end of this reconnaissance, we still had not reached the ice-cap, so I returned with our strongest team to force a route.

Crossing the second ice-fall

We found a route up the right bank of the glacier, which proved easier than expected, and then followed a line of weakness through the middle ice-falls to the left bank. We climbed up and down over a series of pressure waves, and through the difficult crevassed section, in which it was easy to be forced off route. Once across the glacier we were surprised to find a relatively easy route up the edge to the snow line, where we found a rock outcrop suitable for the advanced base camp, at 914 metres.

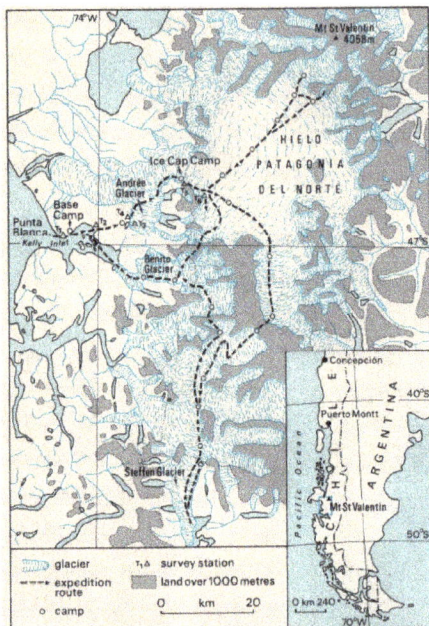

Map showing expedition routes

*Bad weather prohibited survey work for forty-six days and
reduced the area covered, but revised maps will be produced.
Captain Jon Zorijack working at station No. 6*

By the time HMS *Endurance*, the Royal Navy's Antarctic Patrol ship, steamed into the inlet five weeks later we had found the route to the ice-cap. We established a camp, provisionally marked the sites for the next four survey stations and fixed the position of the first triangulation station by astronomical observation. When HMS *Endurance* arrived, we had the worst weather to date on the expedition, but despite this her helicopters flew four tons of food and stores up onto the ice-cap.

Set-back in the survey

Now the survey work really began with Jon Zorijack occupying the second position, while Chris Gobey remained at the start point. All angles were measured by theodolite, the distances by tellurometer and the stations marked. We leap-frogged Chris Gobey to Trig. 3 at the snout of the Andrée Glacier, measured the line in fine style on two good days, then began to move Jon Zorijack to Trig. 4. Disaster struck in evacuating the second station, which was sited on a hill overlooking Kelly Inlet. All the equipment was left on the raised beach, while the party returned to base camp to collect some batteries for the tellurometer. It was spring tide, rising higher than ever over all the equipment and flooding the tellurometer, which was useless thereafter.

Despite this set-back, which lost us three days of sunshine we continued the survey. Instead of using the tellurometer, we used a steel tape and the subtense method, whereby the surveyor lays out a base line at right angles to the line being measured. All the angles are measured which, with the base distance, means the length of the line between stations can be calculated. It is not as accurate as a tellurometer, but in an area where there is no survey, it is at least something.

Without much difficulty, we measured the next leg up the Andrée Glacier, but from here we had to carry the line up to 1160 metres on the ice-cap, over a distance of nine kilometres. Carrying the survey equipment up onto the ice-cap proved a problem and it was six days before the first ice-cap survey station was occupied and ready to measure the line. This was completed the next day, despite poor visibility.

Those of us on the ice-cap then helped to bring up the lower station. For the last week we had bad, very bad weather with strong winds, rain and sleet. All the equipment and personal clothing was sodden. The whole expedition forgathered again for the first time in three weeks, on Boxing Day in our base camp. We took a few days off to reorganize, rest and dry out.

The plan was now to carry the survey via two stations into the upper corries of the Benito Glacier, from where the traverse would be returned to the Kelly Inlet. But before continuing with the survey I wished to make an attempt on Mt San Valentin (4058 metres) the highest mountain in Patagonia. We set off on January 2, with snow falling, to sledge the twenty-six kilometres to the mountain. Four days later, with snow still falling, we reached the foot of the mountain. We stayed seven days below the peak trying to climb it but blizzards and cloud made route-finding in the ice-fall impossible. In spite of this disappointment, the journey was a success because the geologist discovered metasedimentary rocks, which were part of the old roofing material of the north Patagonian granite batholith. These were sandstones with fossils, calcites and gneiss, all of which, when analysed will give valuable information of the early geology of the area.

Waiting for good weather

After the attempt on Mt San Valentin, we returned to reoc-cupy the next two survey stations on the ice-cap at 1200 metres. However, the next fifteen days of continuously bad weather stopped any further survey. The surveyors remained on the sta-tions, waiting for the weather to clear. Finally two days of good weather allowed us to measure the line, take the necessary pan-oramic photographs, and horizontal and vertical angles into all the peaks, thus fixing their relative positions.

Bad visibility and difficult terrain forced us to abandon the sur-vey in favour of other sciences. While the geologist returned to his volcanic rocks in the inlet, the glaciologist to his stakes and snow pits on the Benito Glacier. Sergeant Peter Breadmore, Corporal John Banks and I set off to cross the ice-cap and explore the region of the Steffen Glacier. We sledged for seventeen days covering 209 kilometres down to the southern part of the ice-cap, which has never been explored. This was a preliminary reconnaissance, so that future expeditions would have some idea of the southern terrain, its topography and scientific potential. We rejoined the rest of the expedition in the Kelly Inlet in late February, where we remained working until evacuated by HMS *Endurance* almost a month later.

We were the first party to attempt a major survey in the area, which unfortunately we did not complete as we had planned. But despite the bad weather and difficult terrain much was achieved. We made the first accurate astronomical position fix in the area, fixed six other survey positions to fourth order standard, and taken enough panoramic photographs to revise the maps of the region at the scale of 1:250,000.

Stakes sunk ten metres into the ice were used to measure speed of glacier movement and ablation rates. Lieutenant Martin Sessions uses a steam drill on the Benito Glacier

Annual rainfall is very high, rising from 4500 millimetres at sea level to 7500 millimetres on the ice-cap. Senior Aircraftsman Bill Skelson takes meteorological readings

The expedition also surveyed Kelly Inlet. Echo sounding team spent more than twenty days sounding lines 100 metres apart across the inlet as the basis for a chart

In 1992, Vanessa Winchester and Stephan Harrison together with team members from Operation Raleigh[06] made a route from the southside of Laguna San Rafael to Glacier San Quintin in the vicinity of Co Yañez. They were the first to climb that summit, first depicted on the Royal Navy chart of 1830 and photographed by Nils Pallin and Allan Bäckman in 1921 [Map of Routes of Glacier San Quintin and Kelly Inlet, route 4]. Stephan Harrison returned in 1993 with Operation Raleigh support to ascend Rio Nevado after crossing from Laguna San Rafael to Rio Negro in the partially completed canal cutting [Map of Routes of Glacier San Quintin and Kelly Inlet, route 5].

A summary of the expeditions is provided below by Stephan Harrison.

Travels to the San Quintin Glacier in 1992 and 1993

In the austral summer of 1991 I, along with my colleague Dr Vanessa Winchester, started to research the geomorphology and evolution of the Laguna San Rafael and its calving glacier. This work was supported logistically by Operation Raleigh (now called Raleigh International). At the end of the expedition, we started making plans to undertake similar research on the San Quintin Glacier, to the south of Laguna San Rafael.

As a result, in early 1992 Vanessa and I, along with a group of Raleigh venturers, crossed the Laguna by Zodiac and set up a camp on the southern shore of the Laguna. The next day we moved south-southwest through heavy vegetation and swamps. We crossed the large, wooded lateral moraine complex (which we assessed as similar to the Tempanos moraine fringing the Laguna San Rafael) in the late afternoon and reached the shore of the Rio Blanco that evening. As is usual with proglacial rivers, it was too fast-flowing to cross. We decided therefore to wait until morning when the flow had reduced. The next day therefore we crossed the river, which was about 60 m wide at this time and a metre deep in places. My feet became extremely cold and I pulled a muscle when walking towards the shore which affected my movement for a few days afterwards.

Later that day we camped on the northern lateral moraines of the San Quintin glacier with good access to the glacier. We spent the next week or so on measuring lichens on rock surfaces and taking tree cores for tree-ring analysis to begin to assess the recent fluctuations of this northern part of the glacier. At this time the glacier was close to its lateral moraines. Now it has retreated so quickly that the glacier is currently over 2 km narrower than in 1991 and access to the glacier from our camp would now be impossible without boats. We quite quickly realised that we would not be able to reach the western terminus of the glacier and so the seeds were planted for a further expedition to the glacier terminus.

As a result, in 1993 I organised an expedition supported with Raleigh venturers to gain access to the western and southern terminus part of the glacier and its large terminal moraines. Sadly, Vanessa was unable to join this trip. The logistics of this was much more complicated than the 1992 expedition, because of the much greater distances involved and the difficulties of getting through the extensive swamps and rivers which guarded the north-western and western sides of the glacier. As a result, it was decided that we needed to carry two boats, a Zodiac and a smaller former Special Boat Service recce boat.

The Zodiac was going to be used to ferry people and equipment along the Pacific shoreline from the mouth of the Rio San Tadeo to the mouth of the Rio Nevado which drains the SW terminus of the glacier. The SBS boat was then going to be carried upriver to a camp near the large terminal moraines, to be used to cross the large rivers and ponds in the approaches to the glacier. To deliver two boats to the mouth of the Rio Nevado and then to the Rio San Tadeo plus people, food, tents and supplies, fuel and engine for the Zodiac required an enormous amount of work and time. As a result, Raleigh decided that the expedition was going to be six weeks long (a 'double-phase') and it ended up being the most difficult expedition that Raleigh had ever supported.

Unfortunately, things did not go to plan. The breakers on the shore meant that using the Zodiac to transport equipment and people the 16km or so to the mouth of the Rio Nevado was not possible. It was decided that we would have to carry the recce boat and all our food, tents, etc., along the beach. This was a very difficult undertaking, requiring multiple carries over a number of days.

Eventually, a team of four of us were deposited with tents at the mouth of the Rio Nevado. We then spent a very long, hard day in heavy rain and with heavy rucksacks trying to make our way to find a suitable campsite just to the west of the large terminal moraines and on the northern shore of the river. We accomplished this, although one of the team who had many years' experience of wild camping, mountaineering and ocean canoeing said that it was the hardest day of his life. Eventually, some days later, all the team plus the recce boat were gathered at the camp. Another half day enabled me and a small team to force our way along the southern bank of the river through the large terminal moraine and to the glacier snout. We were surprised to see that it was advancing into vegetated ground and one could step from long grass onto glacial ice within a few metres.

The next few days were spent coring the largest trees on the moraine to obtain some idea of the moraine's likely age. I also spent some time on the glacier and crossed to its southern flank on my own to view the ground to the south. One unusual characteristic of the glacier at this time was that crevasses showed water running from the terminus area up glacier (i.e. from west to east). This is counter to what we had expected. It's difficult to account for this, but it may be that as the glacier was advancing into vegetated ground it might have developed a small forebulge in front of it.

These are common in front of many large glaciers and represent land being squeezed from underneath the glacier towards the terminus region. This water flooding sub-glacially into the centre of the glacier may partially account for its recent rapid recession and break up. From our expedition in early 1993, the glacier terminus has now retreated around 2.5km and currently calves into a lake.

Although the expedition lasted around 6 weeks, we only managed to spend about 5 days on the glacier and its moraines. The rest of the time was taken to move 12 people, two boats, a 40hp engine, around 700kg of fuel, food for 6 weeks and 6 tents through deep swamps some 23km to the Pacific shore from the Laguna San Rafael, and a further 16km along the beach and back. Nearly all of this was accomplished on foot. It was a hard trip, marred by extremely wet weather (it rained on every day but two) but it was also life-changing for me. Not only did I reach the San Quintin glacier for the second time (and perhaps we were the first to reach its terminus) but I also met Tessa Kingsley at our beach camp who was working at Operation Raleigh and had travelled down to the Pacific during a resupply phase. We were married in 1997, and now live with our three children in west Cornwall.

The Winchester and Harrison Expeditions provided valuable information on the recent (200 year) history of the advances of Glacier San Quintin, by dating the trees growing on the many moraines that surround the glacier[07]. Of particular interest was a significant terminal moraine that marks the edge of the glacier's emerging proglacial lake that is dated to 1921. The Professor's expedition most likely witnessed some results of the advance that created the 1921 terminal moraine at Eagle Valley Camp and other sites along the southern edge of the glacier[08].

Martin Sessions, a member of the 1972/73 expedition, was determined to undertake repeat measurements of the surface of Glacier Benito (the South Glacier named by Nils Pallin on his map). In 2007, he led a 12-man international expedition that based itself on the beach at Isla Boscosa in Kelly Inlet, opposite to the Professor's base camp. Over the course of the month, they made a route to Glacier Benito, undertook some measurements that showed the glacier was thinning fast (about 130 metres in 35 years). They returned to Kelly Inlet before being lifted out by the Huemules based out of Tortel, owned by J C Szydlowski [Map of Routes of Glacier San Quintin and Kelly Inlet, route 6][09].

Glacier Benito Revisited 2007. Left to right – Jammie, Olaf, Michael, Vanessa, Martin, Stuart, Steph, Megan, Garth, Aase and Suzie

On the day they arrived in Kelly Inlet, they met the lone canoeist, Cristian Denoso, who was making the first canoe trip around the North Patagonian Icefield. Cristian Denoso had come north from Rio Baker using an inland route that maximised the fjords and low passes between the fjords including coming up Rio Benito and down Rio Andrée [Map of Routes of Glacier San Quintin and Kelly Inlet, route 7]. He went to Laguna San Rafael by using the emerging proglacial lake surrounding the terminus of Glacier San Quintin.

The next documented trips were by the explorer Jarek Wieczorek, under the adventure name Antofaya Expeditions, who used pack rafts to travel up and down rivers and across the many lakes and inlets[10]. Jarek Wieczorek and fellow expeditioners crossed Kelly Inlet many times, but in 2011 and 2018 made their way up to Glacier Andrée and its proglacial lake, following the Professor's route then returning by paddling down Rio Andrée [Map of Routes of Glacier San Quintin and Kelly Inlet, route 8].

In 2011, Martin Sessions returned to Kelly Inlet with Olaf Wündrich and Peter Dowling to make fresh measurements on Glacier Benito[09]. This time, they use packrafts to travel from Laguna San Rafael, where they were dropped off by the ever-helpful Chilean Navy, across the canal cutting down the Rio Negro and Rio San Tadeo, along the ocean beach to Kelly Inlet on their way to the glacier. They were unable to achieve the primary objective of resurveying a six kilometre transept on Glacier Benito at 900 metres above sea level but were able to improve the survey of the lower part of the glacier. This would be the last time anyone could walk from land near the terminus of the glacier on to the glacier itself.

Glacier Benito Revisited 2011. Left to right –
Martin, Olaf and Peter with their packrafts

In 2017, Martin Sessions returned with a six-man team by helicopter from Coyhaique to a site 850 metres above sea level on Glacier Benito. The aim was to repeat the six-kilometre transept. They established that the glacier had thinned by 130 metres in 43 years at this crossing[11]. As the helicopter was going to fly over the route taken by the Professor, Nils Pallin and Allan Bäckman 97 years earlier, the opportunity was taken to fly around Stortoppen and Knallhatten twice to take photographs similar to those taken by Nils and Allan [Map of Routes of Glacier San Quintin and Kelly Inlet, position 9]. Some of these photographs have been used to illustrate 'The Changes' below.

Glacier Benito Revisited 2017. Left to right –
Johnny, Olaf, Martin, Mark, Marcos and Rodrigo their pilot

✧
THE CHANGES
Compiled and written by Martin Sessions

Introduction

Allan Bäckman considered that the metrological data that he recorded was the most valuable outcome from the expedition, as the survey work and glaciological studies had been affected severely by wet weather and equipment problems. In retrospect, the photographs taken by the Professor, Nils Pallin and Allan Bäckman are probably the most valuable record. Little did they realise, as indeed Martin Sessions did not realise in 1973, that climate change was going to wreck havoc on this amazing snow and ice covered region. A few examples of the dramatic changes are illustrated below.

Smutsudden (The Dirt Cape)/Outcrop 245

As the 1920 expedition approached Kelly Inlet onboard the *Yañez*, they photographed San Tadeo Glacier. One feature they did not see was an outcrop on the south side of the glacier that was named Outcrop 245 as that is the altitude of its summit. However, they did see the effect of this 'buried' outcrop on the glacier which was to produce a medial moraine that they photographed from several different places.

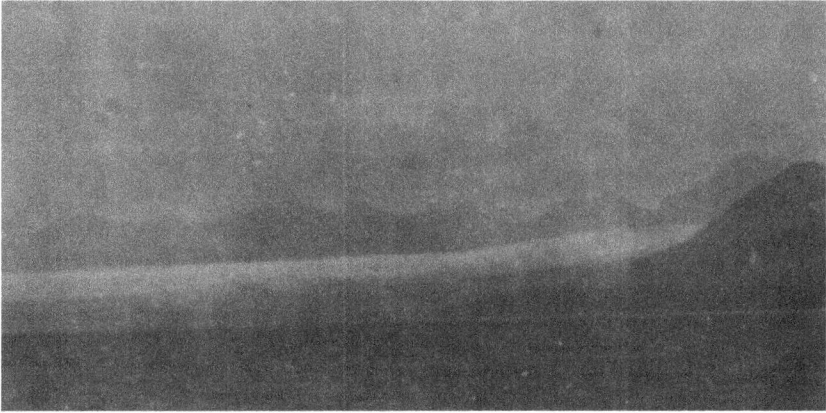

*Enlarged view of part of Glacier San Quintin terminus in 1920/21
from the south-west*

Of interest is the fact that Commander Stokes did not identify this feature on his chart of the coastline in 1828 either, although HMS *Beagle* passed down the coast by only a few kilometres off shore as shown by the depth soundings. The surveyors did identify an estuary, Estr Guapeotao, that was also shown in Garcia's chart of 1768 (refer Note 09 of Prologue). The satellite photograph below of Glacier San Quintin terminus or tongue has superimposed on it the shape of the glacier from the 1830 Royal Navy chart surveyed by HMS *Beagle* and associated ships. Also shown is the 1921 terminal moraine identified by Vanessa Winchester and Stephan Harrison as well as a small portion of the 1850 terminal moraine.

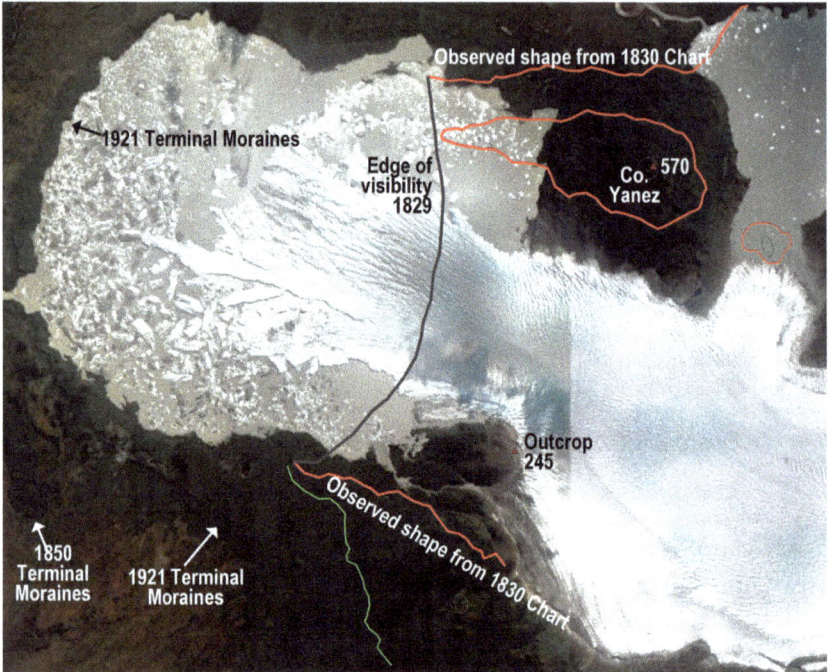

Outline of Glacier San Quintin shown in the 1830 chart superimposed on Google Earth image

The 1944 aerial photograph of Glacier San Quintin terminus from the west shows the medial moraine (Smutsudden or Dirt Cape) being generated by the 'buried' Outcrop 245. An icefall can be seen to the south of the medial moraine. It also shows the nunataks to the east of Co Yañez on the left.

1944 aerial photograph of Glacier San Quintin terminus from the west

In 1972, Outcrop 245 was emerging although it was over-topped by ice.

Glacier San Quintin from the Aquilla *in November 1972*

Glacier San Quintin from the old outwash plain in 1973

By 2011, the Outcrop 245 was very prominent and indeed the glacier tongue on the south side of the rock had almost disappeared.

Glacier San Quintin from the Golfo de San Esteban beach in 2011

The Mud Flats of Kelly Inlet

Numerous photographs were taken by the Swedish expeditioners of the mud flats of Kelly Inlet. As time went on, they were flooded less frequently as more of the water from Glacier Benito flowed south to Benito Inlet and less into the Andreé River.

Mud flats of Kelly Inlet in 1921

By 1972 the mud flats rarely flooded

In 2017, no evidence of recent flooding existed

Glaciers Andrée (the Kelly Glacier) and Frœnkel

The change in the glaciers Andrée and Frænkel as viewed from the route to Knalhatten is so dramatic that Glacier Andrée is no longer visible from this route.

*Glaciers Andrée and Frænkel as photographed by
the Swedish expeditioners in 1920*

All that can be seen is a small part of Glacier Frænkel in 2017.

The 'empty' valley of Glacier Andrée and Glacier Frænkel
as photographed from the helicopter in 2017

Co Yañez

The first photograph here was taken of Co Yañez on the route from Kelly Inlet to Eagle Valley Camp in 1921. A similar photograph taken from a helicopter 97 years later shows of dramatic change in thickness of Glacier San Quintin.

Co Yañez on the far side of Glacier San Quintin
photographed by Nils Pallin in 1920

Co Yañez on the far side of Glacier San Quintin
photographed near Knallhatten in 2017

The Nunatak of Glacier San Quintin

In 1920, a nunatak was just visible above the glacier on the
north side. In 2017, it is no longer a nunatak.

A nunatak to the East of Co Yañez on the far side of Glacier San Quintin
photographed by Nils Pallin in 1920

The same rock feature to the east of Co Yañez
on the far side of Glacier San Quintin in 2017

Glacier Benito (the South Glacier) from Kelly Inlet

In 1920, Glacier Benito was distinctly visible from Kelly Inlet. Less of the glacier could be seen as time progressed such that, based on the latest satellite photographs, it is no longer visible from Kelly Inlet.

Glacier Benito (South Glacier) in 1920

Glacier Benito from Kelly Inlet in 2007

Glacier Benito from Kelly Inlet in 2011

Glacier Rabot

Nils Pallin named Glacier Rabot after Charles Rabot, a famous French Explorer, who was with the Professor during the expeditions to Tierra del Fuego in 1890s. This glacier was a significant offshoot from Glacier Benito in 1920.

Glacier Rabot photographed by Nils Pallin in 1920

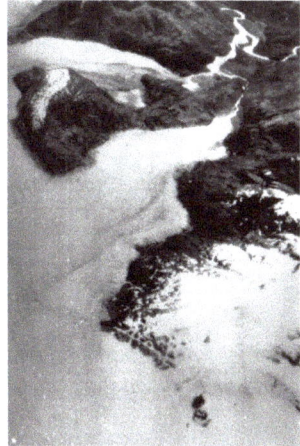

Glacier Rabot from a 1944
USAF aerial photograph

Glacier Rabot photographed from the summit of Co. Caldenius in 1973

The valley that Glacier Rabot used to occupy
photographed from a drone above the summit of Co. Caldenius in 2017

Glacier Rabot should have been between the bare Co Caldenius on the left and the bare hill on the right. All one can see now is the rapidly thinning Glacier Benito between the two peaks (2017)

Final Thoughts

Whilst there have been over 10,000 'summits' of Mount Everest since 1920, no one other than the members of Professor Nordenskjöld's Swedish South America expedition have crossed from Kelly Inlet to Glacier San Quintin, no one has taken photographs from Knallhatten and no one has walked on Glacier San Quintin where the Professor, Nils Pallin and Allan Bäckman walked. Indeed, no one is likely to walk on Glacier San Quintin where they did because the ice is no longer there.

Of the five glaciers named by Nils Pallin on his map in Chapter 7, two have now vanished.

✧
Notes and Observations
PROLOGUE

01. Dates differ in different reports due to a change to the Gregorian calendar. England did not adopt the Gregorian calendar until 1752.

02. See en.wikipedia.org/wiki/George_Anson 32s_voyage_around_the_world and en.wikipedia.org/wiki/Wager_Mutiny

03. "Byron's Narrative of the Loss of the Wager", Bradbury and Evans, 1832. Harvard University Library Copy digitised by Google books.

04. 'The adventures of Capt. Cheap, the Hon. Mr. Byron, Lieut. Hamilton, Alexander Campbell and others, late of his Majesty's Ship the Wager, which was wrecked on a desolate island in Lat. 47. S. Long. 81. 40. W. in the South Seas, in the year 1741', Alexander Campbell. Refer https://patlibros.org/mac/index.php?lan=eng.

05. 'Descripcion Historial de la Provincia y Archipieago de Chiloe, . . . '. Padre Fray Pedro Gonzalez de Agueros. 1791. Page 282 describes the visit to Estero Jesuitas together with Benito Inlet and Julian Inlet by Pilot Don Pedro (although the specific place names are not mentioned here).

06. 'Patagonia Occidental – Las Cordilleras Patagonicas y sus Regiones Circundantes por Dr. Hans Steffen', Eugenio Aspillage Fontaine & Luis Catalan Torres Editors, University of Chile 1944.

07. 'Expediciones Hidrograficas En La Zona De Chiloe', Capitán de Navío Hernán Ferrer Fougá. Task undertaken by the Author during the Journeys in the Region of Chiloé, made between the days 3 to the 7 of November of 1986, under the auspices of the Institute of Research of the Heritage Territorial of Chile.

08. 'Cannons of the Wager, a Formal Find for Historical Archaeology in Gulfo de Penas' (Tuesday, April 17, 2012, by Radio Natalesand Ramón Arriagada) http://sociedaddebibliofiloschilenos.blog-spot.com/2512/04/canones-de-la-wager-un-hallazgo.html

09. The chart below is an extract of a chart that was reproduced in the Anuario Hidrográfico de la Marina de Chile Volume 14 (1889). The original chart was drawn in 1768 for Fr Jose Garcia to show his missionary journeys of 1766 and 1767. Modern names have been added where appropriate. The phrase 'Acá se perdió un navío' indicates where the *Wager* was lost.

Fr Jose Garcia's Chart of 1768

10. All maps have been created from MapCarta and Google Maps and subsequently modified with additional place names.

11. See en.wikipedia.org/wiki/Indigenous_peoples_in_Chile and other sources.

12. 'Historical records of San Rafael glacier advances (North Patagonian Icefield): another clue to "Little Ice Age" timing in southern Chile?', Alberto Areneda et al, The Holocene 17,7 (2007) pp. 987–998.

13. 'Reconstructing Four Centuries of Temperature-Induced Coral Bleaching on the Great Barrier Reef', Nicholas A. Kamenos and Sebastian J. Hennige, Frontiers in Marine Science, 15 August 2018.

14. en.wikipedia.org/wiki/1815_eruption_of_Mount_Tambora and en.wikipedia.org/wiki/Year_Without_a_Summer

15. en.wikipedia.org/wiki/1808_mystery_eruption

16. Pringle Stokes's final hand-written journal is in the New South Wales State Library. G Ingleton purchased the journal from a descendant of Governor King in a dirty and deplorable condition including many external parts eaten by rats! The refurbishment of the journal was completed in 1979. P P King used the journal to write his Volume 1 to "Narrative of the Surveying Voyages of His Majesty's Ships Adventure and Beagle . ." See Note 17 below. With acknowledgement to the New South Wales State Library.

17. Captain P P King in Volume 1 of 'Narrative of the Surveying Voyages of His Majesty's Ships Adventure and Beagle . . .' paraphrased Stokes's original journal extensively, in the process losing some of the raw impact of the original writings. See 'Narrative of the Surveying Voyages of His Majesty's Ships Adventure and Beagle between the years 1831 and 1836 . . .', Volume 1, 'Proceedings of the First Expedition, 1831-1830, under the command of Captain P. Parker King, R.N., F.R.S', London: Henry Colburn 1839.

18. Kelly Inlet, also known as Bahia (or Estero) Chacualat. Agueros, Steffen, Captain King and others do not mention the name Bahia Chacualat, and Steffen's books were published in 1909 and 1948. A Royal Navy chart from 1888 titled *Gulf of Penas to Guaytecas Islands* does show Bahia Chacualat as the alternative name for

Kelly Inlet. This chart incorporated Chilean Government surveys of 1870-3, which would have included Enrique Simpson's work of the first proper survey Laguna San Rafael. However, the chart drawn of Fr Jose Garcia (see Note 09 above) shows Chagualat in the same position as the Jesuit Sound and indeed there is also a Punta Chagualat on the north coast of Golfo de Penas. It appears that Bahia Chacualat is in the wrong place and is spelt wrongly.

19. Benedictus Marwood Kelly was born on 3rd February 1785 and entered the Royal Navy as a midshipman aged 13. After an eventful few years, he was promoted to lieutenant on 13 January 1806. By 28 November 1811, he advanced to commander. After a spell on half-pay, on 28 September 1818, he was appointed to command the *Pheasant* of 22 guns off the west coast of Africa on anti-slavery patrols. He returned to half pay in February in 1822 on grounds of ill health following his service in the tropics. His most outstanding feat (and there were many) was his revelation of the brutality of the slave trade off West Africa in 1820, which went on to influence Queen Victoria and Prince Albert's stance on the subject. Clearly, he was a man of influence which was why he 'petitioned' Captain P P King to have Commander Pringle Stokes as the Captain of HMS *Beagle*. He probably did this whilst he was in the City of London after 1822 where he could meet with his friends and acquaintances at the Admiralty. He was also a man of vision investing in firstly the railways, then the new steam ships and finally telegraphs. For a full statement on his life, refer to https://www.saltfordenvironmentgroup.org.uk/history/history010.html .

20. Glacier San Quintin (also known originally as Glacier San Tadeo). See File:ISS047-E-128046 - View of Earth.jpg - Wikimedia Commons for a great view of this region of interest from space. Glacier San Quintin is the largest glacier flowing from the icefield.

21. en.wikipedia.org/wiki/Robert_FitzRoy

22. 'Narrative of the Surveying Voyages of His Majesty's Ships Adventure and Beagle between the years 1831 and 1836 . . .',

Volume 3, 'Journal and Remarks. 1832—1836. By Charles Darwin, Esq., M.A. sec. Geol. Soc.'

23. Page 334 of Volume 1, 'Proceedings of the First Expedition, 1831-1830, under the command of Captain P. Parker King, R.N., F.R.S'.

24. What Mr Kirke saw of the large glacier from Benito Inlet is shown below in a photograph taken in 2009 by Jarek Wieczorek of Antofaya Expeditions (with acknowledgement). In the foreground is Glacier Andrée flowing from the large glacier (Glacier San Quintin) behind. The level of ice would have been over 100 meters higher and the exposed rock in the Glacier Andrée would not have been visible in 1830.

View of glaciers Andrée and San Quintin from Benito Inlet in 2009 (acknowledgement Jarek Wieczorek)

25. 'Chart of the South West Coast of South America from Latitude 46° 34› to 47° 47› South. Surveyed in the years 1828 & 1830 in H M Sloop Beagle and Adelaide Tender under the orders of Commander P P King, H M S Adventure'. 1830. G223 Shelf Ft. With acknowledgement to UK Hydrographic Office, Taunton.

26. 'Recent Oscillations of the San Quintin and San Rafael Glaciers, Patagonian Chile', Vanessa Winchester and Stephan Harrison, Geografiska Annaler 76 A (1996).

27. 'Vajes de Esploracion i Estudio en la Patagonia Occidental 1892-1902' Volume 2, Dr. Hans Steffen, University de Chile, Imprenta Obrvantes, 1910.

    Translated pages are from 314 to 317 with the translation provided by Olaf Wündrich.

28. *Estero* – estuary, a section of a river of great width and flow that has been invaded by the sea due to the influence of the tides and the sinking of the banks; in some large sludge deposits accumulate, while others remain relatively free due to the effect of the receding tide.

29. *penas* - means sorrows, whereas peñas means rock cliffs or rocks. With time the ñ became an n and the rocks became sorrows of many explorer. Officially it is Golfo de Penas in recent charts.

30. *vega* - low, flat, fertile land and generally on the banks of a river.

31. Also known as *tepa*.

32. *Chusquea quila - perennal bamboo.*

33. *Laureliopsis philippiana.*

34. *Nothofagus obliqua.*

35. Cíprés de las Guaitecas.

36. Igneous rock composed essentially of feldspar and amphibolite.

37. Dark green metamorphic rock of great hardness.

38. Cíprés de las Guaitecas.

39. Numerous references exist online describing the German East Asia Squadron, Battle of Coronel and the Battle of the Falkland Islands. Online references used here are:

    The Pepper Treader by Geoffrey Bennett

    Military History, Castles of Steel, Chapter 13 by Robert K Massie

    War and Security, Coronel to the Falkland Islands 1914, by Martin Gibson

40. First attempt to build Cabo Raper lighthouse was in 1900. Work was restarted in 1910 and completed by 1914. See Wikipedia - https://es.wikipedia.org/wiki/Faro_Cabo_Raper.

CHAPTER 1

01. Sources are:
    - https://en.wikipedia.org/wiki/Otto_Nordenskjöld
    - Dictionary of Falklands Biography including South Georgia by David Tatham (https://www.falklandsbiographies.org/biographies/346)
    - Nature, Hugh Robert Mill, No. 3061, Vol. 121, June 30, 1928, page 1026

02. Otto Nordenskjöld's 1896-97 expedition to the Southern Icefield of the Chilean Andes.

03. For detailed reports on this expedition, refer to *Antarctic Challenges – Historical and Current Perspectives on Otto Nordenskjöld's Antarctic Expedition 1901-1903*. Christian Hjort and Ólafur Ingólfsson, Gothenburg: Royal Soc. Of Arts and Sciences, 2004.

    An excellent video of this expedition is available at

    https://www.abc.net.au/catalyst/otto-Nordenskjöld/11011932.

04. 'En resa i Sydlamerikas Kordillerastater' by Otto Nordenskjöld. Lecture to the Swedish Society for Anthropology and Geography, November 18, 1921. YMER 1921. H. 3 O, 4·

05. https://sv.m.wikipedia.org/wiki/Nils_Pallin

06. Image kindly supplied by Unn Hellsten, Åsa Hellsten, and Ulf Hellsten

07. Compiled by Johan Grönberg from:

    SVENSKA DAGBLADET 18 Mar 1939

    SVENSKA DAGBLADET 26 Mar 1939

    SVENSKA DAGBLADET 28 Mar 1939

    SONDERHAMNS TIDNING 9 Nov 1939

08. Compiled by Johan Grönberg from:

    Allan Bäckman CV

    SVENSKA DAGBLADET 30 Aug 1956

    SVENSKA DAGBLADET 1 Sep 1956 (x 2)

CHAPTER 2

01. Translation from Swedish made in 2019/20 by Unn Hellsten, Åsa Hellsten, Ulf Hellsten. H N Pallin's grandchildren. Subsequently edited to improve readability in English.

02. The passenger train route south to Puerto Montt fell into disrepair by 1992 (assisted by earthquake damage). It has been repaired subsequently but is not open to passenger trains.

03. *Yañez* was built by J.T. Eltringham, South Shields for the Goole & Hull Steam Towing Co., Goole in 1882. Its displacement was 131 tonnes and length was 100 feet. The hull was iron and the ship had propeller propulsion. The 400 IHP engine was triple expansion built by J.P. Rennold Sons & Co., South Shields giving a maximum speed of 10 knots. Acquired in 1895 and served as a cutter at the Talcahuano Naval Station. It later served as a passenger transport to the Quiriquina island. Her service was terminated in 1936. (https://en.wikipedia.org/wiki/List_of_decommissioned_ships_of_the_Chilean_Navy)

04. In Spanish, known as Abra Kelly and in English known as Kelly Inlet.

05. Three indigenous peoples occupied Chiloé. The Cuncos and Huilliches who were settled and lived off the land using agriculture and the Chonos who were nomadic and travelled as far south as the Golfo de Penas via the Istmo de Ofqui using their special canoes (*dalcas*) that could be taken apart to traverse the isthmus. The Spanish arrived in 1558 and took possession of the island. Because visits from other Spaniards were probably few and far between due to its remoteness from Peru, the centre of the Spanish empire in South America, a significant intermixing between the inhabitants' languages occurred. Communication between the expeditioners and the Chilotes would have been in Spanish.

06. In more recent maps, the San Tadeo Glacier is known as the San Quintin Glacier (Ventisquero San Quintin).

07. In 1937, work began on constructing the canal from Laguna San Rafael to Rio Negro (Black River). This work continued

until 1943 when funds ran out. Visit https://web.archive.org/web/25125606010900/http://www.railwaysofthefarsouth.co.uk/13jisthmusofofqu.html to view more details including the 'little' railway to transport the excavated material. The cutting is used today as a route to go south from Laguna San Rafael.

08. *Ana Pink* was one of the ships of Commodore Anson's squadron in the early 1740s which also included the *Wager*.

09. There was also a huge 'cipres de las guitecas' woodcutter industry along the coast, maybe unbeknown to the author.

10. Cabo Raper lighthouse was commissioned in 1914. It was initially served by a 3.5 km railway from Seño Hoppner. Cabo Raper has weather records going back to 1912. See http://www.railwaysofthefarsouth.co.uk/13elighthouses.html?LMCL=IldPh0.

11 See Epilogue for changes in Glacier San Quintin terminus or 'snout'.

12. 'Narrative of the Surveying Voyages of His Majesty's Ships *Adventure* and *Beagle* between the years 1831 and 1836 . . .', Volume 1, 'Proceedings of the First Expedition, 1831-1830, under the command of Captain P. Parker King, R.N., F.R.S', London: Henry Colburn 1839.

13. Extracts from Allan Bäckman's letters to his wife, Elna, were kindly provided for inclusion by John Hendeström, grandson of Allan, in Swedish. They were translated using 'Google translate' then selectively edited for context. The letters were in a diary format. Note that the tense changes in these letters in diary form depending on whether he was describing events, his thoughts or future activities.

14. Allan and Sten participated in the first part of the 1920-21 Swedish Expedition to South America which centred around Peru so had much experience in the 'jungles' of that region including the headwaters of rivers leading to the Amazon.

15. The chart (map) of Kelly Inlet was based on Commander Stokes brief survey of the inlet in 1828 and would have not been updated since that survey, 92 years later.

CHAPTER 3

01. The 1972/73 British Services Expedition to Chilean Patagonia, based in Kelly Inlet had a song to illustrate this (acknowledgement to Jonathan Zorichak):

> *When you grow old,*
> *You may be told,*
> *Of an expedition very bold,*
> *Of hand picked men,*
> *With lots of brains,*
> *Who went to a land,*
> *Where it always rains.*
> *Don't take no baloney,*
> *It was hell in Patagoni,*
> *Oh it's great to remeniski,*
> *Just give me lots more whisky!*

02. Photographs and maps that appeared in H N Pallin's article in the *Alpine Journal* titled 'Mountains And Glaciers In West Patagonia', published in No. 45, 1933 are indicated with [AJ] and are acknowledged accordingly.

03. The glaciers are the Andrée Glacier (Ventisquero Andrée) which Pallin has called the Kelly Glacier here and the Benito Glacier which he has shown as the South Glacier (Ventisquero del Sur) in the Map in Chapter 7. Outlet rivers from the Benito Glacier flowed both into Benito Inlet to the south and the Andrée River to the west. Both glaciers dammed large lakes in the lower Ablation (or melting) zone. Periodically these lakes would have emptied in a dramatic fashion creating severe floods in the southern Kelly Valley (known as Glacial Lake Outburst Flood – GLOF). Another feature of these temperate glaciers is that, whilst they can slide over rock surface smoothly due to water lubrication, broken off rock material becomes embedded in the ice and this material is then ground against the native rock which creates 'rock flour' or colloid in the water. It is this rock flour (sludge) that has coloured the water in Kelly Inlet and created the mud banks.

04. For Mummery-type tents, refer to https://en.wikipedia.org/wiki/ Mummery_tent.

05. Known as Punta Blanca.

06. In his final map published in the *Alpine Journal*, Nils Pallin called this the Andrée Glacier. See Chapter 4 Note 13.

Glacier Andrée from the 'mud' flats in 2007

Last glimpse of Glacier Andrée from Punta Blanca in 2011

07. San Javier when translated to English is Saint Xavier.

Kelly Inlet from a helicopter in 2017 with Punta Blanca on the right and Isla Boscosa surrounded by 'mud' flats.

08. Corned beef is beef that is cooked in brine and then packaged in a can. The name comes from the salt grains, which are used when the meat is prepared, not from 'corn' (corn).

09. Southern beech, a genus of trees and shrubs, which are found in South America, among other places.

CHAPTER 4

01. The Baker Fjord maximum depth is 1,075 metres. The Baker Fjord and Canal Messier share the same 'mouth' and Canal Messier is deeper than Baker Fjord at 1,325 metres. Sognefjord's depth is currently quoted as 1,308 metres.

02. On the Chilean side of the Chile / Argentina border, this lake is called Lago General Carrera. Most of this lake lies within Chile.

03. The North Patagonian Icefield, where Glacier San Tadeo (San Quintin) is located, is smaller than the South Patagonian Icefield.

04. Most likely, Darwin's Falls which is the most obvious waterfalls to be seen in Kelly Inlet. Stokes referred to these falls as the best place to collect drinking water for ships. See Prologue Note 16. In fact, neither Darwin nor Fitz-Roy visited Kelly Inlet.

05. Stortoppen (Big Top - left), the survey point, and Knallhatten (right) taken from a helicopter in 2017. In modern Swedish, 'Knallhatten' translates as the 'Squib' which is a 'firework'. Maybe the Norwegian translation is better – 'Pestle' Hat or more appropriate 'Bowler Hat'.

Stortoppen and Knallhatten in 2017

06. See the photograph titled 'Looking towards the north to Co Yañez and Laguna San Rafael in the far distance behind Co Yañez'. In fact, the 'rather great unknown lake' is probably the flooded outwash area of Glacier San Tadeo, given that the season was summer and the expedition had experienced considerable rain.

07. A cairn or big rock on top of Stortoppen (Big Top) in 2017.

Summit of Stortoppen in 2017

08. The height of Cerro San Valentin is currently 4,033 metres above sea level (EGM 2008).

09. The 1972-1973 British Joint Services Expedition used this route to the main icefield and for a survey line. See Epilogue, 'Map-making on the Patagonian Ice-cap'.

10. The official name of the icefield is El Campo De Hielo Norte or the North Patagonian Icefield.

11. This photograph has an interesting feature as shown below where there is a 'bare' zone in the bottom right hand corner. The river flows in the white area above the bare land.

Glacier Andrée terminus in 1921

A photograph from the 1944 aerial survey illustrate this zone. The view is from the west. The distance from the glacier river (R. Andrée) to the edge of the zone is about 3 kilometres.

Glaciers Andrée and Frænkel in 1944

The zone of interest in a direct line with Glacier Frænkel raises questions:

Did Glacier Frænkel surge before Glacier Andrée advanced? An unstable icefall exists in Glacier Frænkel in the zone between ablation and accumulation (which is part of the main icefield). If a surge did occur, when did it occur?

See Epilogue, the Changes for how much of these two glaciers are visible today.

12. Glacier Rabot was a side glacier flowing from Benito Glacier and was named after Charles Rabot (1856-1944), a French explorer, geographer and mountaineer, who chronicled Professor Nordenskjöld's expeditions to Tierra del Fuego in a book titled 'La Terre de Feu, d'après Otto Nordenskjöld'. This glacier no longer exists due to rapid climate change occurring in this region (refer to Epilogue, the Changes).

13. Glaciers Andrée, Strindberg and Frænkel were named after three Swedish polar explorers. S. A. Andrée was an engineer, aeronaut and polar balloonist. In July 1897, he attempted to fly over the geographic North Pole in a hydrogen-filled balloon with two companions, Nils Strindberg and Knut Frænkel. The balloon crashed on polar ice after only two days. The trio made their way to the deserted Kvitøya (White Island) in Svalbard (Spitsbergen) where they subsequently died. Their remains were found in 1930, causing a media sensation in Sweden (refer https://en.wikipedia.org/wiki/Andr C3 A9e 27s_Arctic_balloon_expedition). Nils Pallin must have completed his map in the *Alpine Journal* article shortly after this event (see Chapter 3, Note 02).

In 1897 Pallin, 17 years old, met Andrée while working in a shipping store in Stockholm where Andrée bought a lot of equipment for his flight. At that time Andrée was very famous. Explorers were stars at that time, not only in Sweden. Later Pallin went to Svalbard and wrote a book about the Andrée riddle in 1932.

The Strindberg glacier no longer exists due to rapid climate change.

14. In the 1921 photograph of Glacier San Tadeo, there is a 'nunatak' (summit is about 440 m above sea level - asl) on the far side of the glacier. Below shows a similar view taken from the helicopter in 2017. Mt San Valentin can be seen in the distance on the right of the photograph.

The former nunatak of Glacier San Quintin in 2017

15. Allan probably means a comparison between the above-mentioned cooking barometer and an aneroid barometer (from Greek for 'without liquid'). This is a barometer designed by the Swede JG Paulin, which consists of an airtight and evacuated flexible metal box, a so-called aneroid box, for use in altimetry. The movement is transferred to a pointer and a scale and the air pressure deformation of the aneroid box is compensated by a spring. For precise measurements, the height above sea level is corrected. The aneroid barometer was originally intended for direct measurement of topographic elevation variations.

16. Battle fought 5-12 September 1914 and which resulted in an Allied victory against the German army and came to create four years of trench warfare on the western front.

17. 'Powdered their peaks' means that light snow has fallen on the surrounding peaks; a frequent occurrence once the cold front has passed through.

18. Clinometer is an instrument that indicates the inclination, i.e. the slope towards a horizontal line or the plumb line.

19. A firer shovelled coal to the boiler, which produced hot steam, which was the energy in the steam locomotive. SJ got its first electric locomotive in 1915. However, in 1920 most SJ locomotives were still powered by steam.

20. Co Yañez (summit 570 m asl) as viewed from a helicopter in 2017. The glacier no longer flows on the far side of Co Yañez. Laguna San Rafael can be seen in the distance beyond Co Yañez. Warm Tarn in Eagle Valley is on the left and Shelf Lake or Rock Tarn is on the right in the foreground. The glacier was near Warm Tarn in 1920.

21. 'Nährungsgebiet' is an old German word seldomly used. Nährungsgebiet means something like 'source of nutrition'. In the glaciology context, it means the accumulation zone, higher up the glacier, where snowfall accumulates and exceeds the losses from ablation.

22. 'Thirteenth evening' is equivalent to the 'Twelfth night' in the English Christmas calendar.

23. Ice equipment comprised of ice axe, crampons and a long rope.

Co Yañez as viewed from a helicopter in 2017

CHAPTER 5

01. In glaciological terms, the 'shoreline' is the trim line which is a clear line on the side of a valley formed by a glacier. The line marks the most recent highest extent of the glacier. In the case of these west-flowing Patagonian glaciers whose lower areas flow through thick forests, it dates to the mid-1850s (to be verified). Pallin estimated here that the surface of the glacier at this point was only 30 metres below its recent (@ 1850) maximum thickness.

02. On the ridge in the distance, the trim line can be seen between the forest and the cleared ground. Eagle Valley camp was on the moraine between the two lakes. This is the only photograph of these glaciers that appeared in Otto Nordenskjöld's book titled *People and Nature in South America (Människor och natur i Sydamerika)*.

03. The Chilotes had assisted gold prospectors and timber merchants in crossing the Istmo de Ofqui in the 1890s and later in their quest for gold and the resistant to decay timber 'ciprés de Guitecas' in the Peninsula de Taitao.

04. Martin Sessions traversing a region of side crevasses on Glacier Benito in 1972. The velocity in the centre of this glacier in this region was about 400 metres a year.

Martin Sessions negotiating a crevasse on Glacier Benito in 1972

05.   Note how close the glacier is to the '1850s' Trim Line on the far
      side of the lake and the fallen trees below the standing trees on
      the far side of the lake. In the archive of Professor Nordenskjold's
      material at the University of Gothenburg, several photographs of
      the edge of the glacier exist. Some examples are included below.

A cliff of ice bordering a glacial lake near some lichen -covered rocks

The same cliff of ice from a different angle showing the glacier near vegetation

Nils Pallin at a glacier-dammed lake

*Photograph shows fresh rock moraine intermingled with
old lichen and moss-covered rocks*

Another photograph in a source album shows Professor
Nordenskjöld standing on possible churned up soil next to 'vir-
gin' forest. This photograph was located with other vegetation
photographs in the vicinity of Kelly Inlet but nothing in this
photograph indicates that it is Kelly Inlet. A guess is that he is
standing near the trim line.

Professor Nordenskjöld in an area of fresh ground damage
next to old vegetation

The expedition observed an advance of the glacier over ground that had been free of ice for a number of years as indicated by the vegetation, moss and lichen. In fact, this advance has been dated by Vanessa Winchester and Stephan Harrison at the glacier terminus to 1921 (see Prologue Note 26 and Epilogue). The advance may have been due to a surface wave travelling down the glacier. Surface waves can travel down the glacier at three to four times faster than the glacier speed, estimated to be about 1 km a year (a, b). The Cabo Raper lighthouse started recording precipitation in 1912. For four months in 1912 the station recorded precipitation of over 300% of the monthly average. In 1913 as a whole, the annual precipitation was over 210% of the monthly average (c). If this significant increase in precipitation also occurred on the icefield with snow cover taking much longer to thaw in the summer, then that precipitation event could have caused a surface wave down the glacier. The surface wave may have taken about nine years to travel down the glacier to create the second largest moraine at the terminus which edges the newly formed pro-glacial lake (refer Prologue Note 26).

References:

a. 'Waves on glaciers', A. C. Fowler, J . Fluid Mech. (1982), vol. 120, p p . 283-321

b. 'Ice motion of the Patagonian Icefields of South America: 1984–2014', J. Mouginot and E. Rignot, AGU, Geophysical Research Letters 10.1002/2014GL062661

c. 'Report on Meteorology. Joint Services Expedition Chilean Patagonia 1972-1973', M P N Sessions, Limited Issue

06. 'Dirt Cape' moraine is associated with an outcrop emerging on the southern side of Glacier San Quintin terminus. See Epilogue.

Another view of the 'Dirt Cape'

*'Dirt Cape' can be seen on the right of this photograph whilst the
Glacier Tongue can be seen in the distance.
Note the vegetation on the ridge on the left*

07. This photograph from a source album shows a pebbly beach in
     front of tangled vegetation. This photograph was located with
     other vegetation photographs from the vicinity of Kelly Inlet
     but nothing in this photograph indicates that it is Kelly Inlet.
     A guess is that it may be associated with the recorded incident
     at Warm Tarn.

Scattered stones and earth against old vegetation

08.   Part of H N Pallin's Map of Eagle Valley has been superimposed
      on a 2016 image from Google Earth (GE). The reference point is
      Warm Tarn (approximately 335 metres asl) and the image from
      the Map has been sized to fit Warm Tarn and orientated on the
      rivers that flow into Warm Tarn. The green contour line would
      be about 350 metres asl which may be about the altitude of the
      trim line.

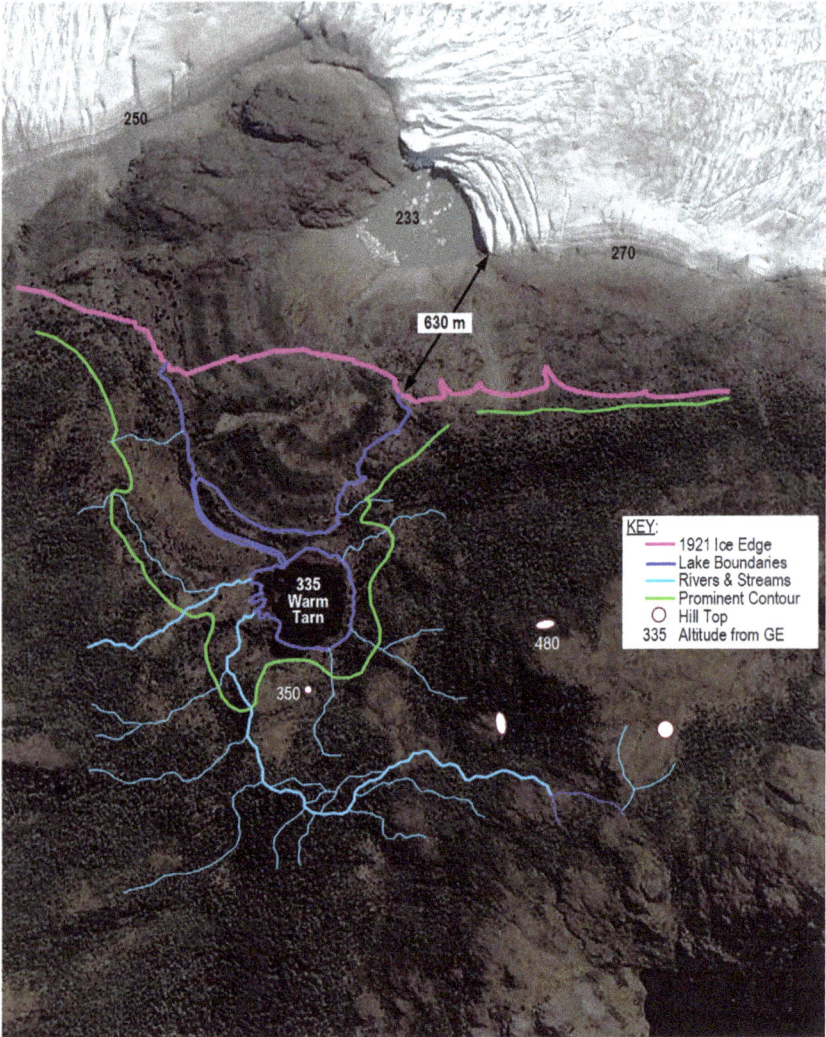

Pallin's map of Eagle Valley superimposed on 2016 image from Google Earth

09. Lago Bäckman in 2016 from Google Earth. In 1921, the lake was dammed by the ice in the middle of the widest part and filled the valley to the bottom right hand corner of the image. Allan named this lake 'Lake Elna' in his diary after his wife.

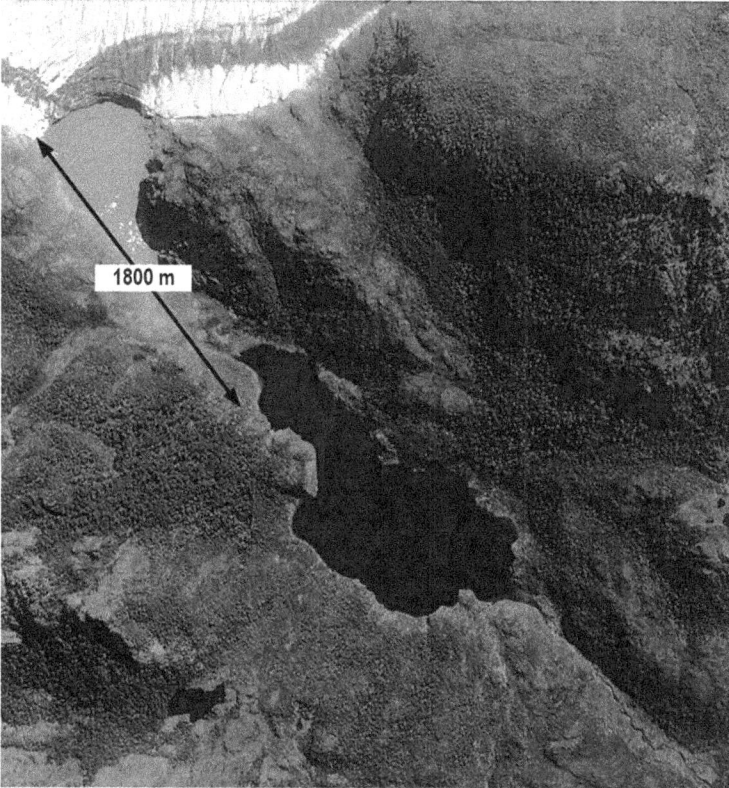

Lago Bäckman in 2016 from Google Earth

10. Further evidence of a recent advance of the glacier. See Note 05 above.
11. The steep, crevassed glacier tongue flowing into Lago Bäckman.

Glacier tongue from Glacier San Quintin flowing into Lago Bäckman

12. Allan uses the word 'sextant' in his diary in several places. This word translates to 'sextant' in English which is the marine instrument for determining one's position using Astro-navigation techniques and does not make sense here. With the marine connotation, one suspects that this may have been a brand name for ship's biscuits or 'hardtack'.

CHAPTER 6

01. Refer to the Epilogue to see how this view has changed.
02. Refer to the Epilogue to see how this view has changed.
03. On the waterways to Glacier Andrée in 1972.

Following in the 'footsteps' of Professor Nordenskjöld in 1972

04. The Wobbly Mirelands in 1972 floating on up to one meter of water.

Walking across the Wobbly Mirelands in 1972

05.   In the bush on the way to Glacier Andrée in 1972.

Transporting supplies to Glacier Andrée in 1972

06.   Early approach view of Glacier Andrée in 1972

First view of Glacier Andrée in 1972

07. A view of the Kelly Glacier taken by the Professor on his way
     north up the west side of the glacier.

West side of Glacier Andrée in 1921

*Looking back towards the river outlet of the glacier in the valley
in the middle of the photograph.*

08.   Sten with his goose with the Kelly Glacier behind him.

Sten with goose in front of Glacier Andrée in 1921

09.   Most likely the Dombey's beech Coigüe (*Nothofagus dombeyi*).
10.   This cypress is from the *Libocedrus* [NZ cedar] genus in New Zealand, which is quite similar but most likely the cypress seen on this expedition is the 'ciprés de Guitecas' (*Pilgerodendron uviferum*)
11.   Another view of Glacier Andrée in 1972.

View of Glacier Andrée with its pro-glacial lake in 1972

12. Glacier Andrée terminus in 1972.

Crossing a river on the way to Glacier Andrée in 1972

A view of Glacier Andrée in 1972 with Glacier Frænkel visible on the right side.

13. Refer to the Epilogue to see how this view has changed.

14. The bird is the Bandurria (Ibis) (*Theristicus melanopis*)

15. The actual island is Isla Guamblin ('old timers' sometimes say Huamblin or Island of Socorro)

16. GÖTEBORGS DAGBLAD half-weekly edition No. 33 dated 27th April 1921

17. Professor Nordenskjöld had lived off seal meat for over two
     years during his Antarctic expedition!

CHAPTER 7

01. 'Narrative of the Surveying Voyages of His Majesty's Ships
     Adventure and *Beagle* between the years 1831 and 1836 . . .',
     Volume 3, 'Journal and Remarks. 1832—1836. By Charles
     Darwin, Esq., M.A. sec. Geol. Soc.'

02. Sources are:
     • https://en.wikipedia.org/wiki/Otto_Nordenskjöld
     • Dictionary of Falklands Biography including South Georgia
       by David Tatham (https://www.falklandsbiographies.org/
       biographies/346)
     • *Nature*, Hugh Robert Mill, No. 3061, Vol. 121, June 30, 1928,
       page 1026
       A recent book on the life of Otto Nordenskjöld mainly in
       photographs titled "Otto Nordenskjöld genom kameran :
       forskningsresorna i bilder" (Otto Nordenskjöld through the
       camera: the research journeys in pictures) by Clas G. Alvstam
       and others, Halvklotband, Svenska, 2021

03. https://sv.m.wikipedia.org/wiki/Nils_Pallin

04. Compiled by Johan Grönberg from:
     SVENSKA DAGBLADET 18 Mar 1939
     SVENSKA DAGBLADET 26 Mar 1939
     SVENSKA DAGBLADET 28 Mar 1939
     SONDERHAMNS TIDNING 9 Nov 1939
     Personal communication from Gothenburg Natural History
     Museum

05. From SVENSKA DAGBLADET 18 Mar 1939

06. Compiled by Johan Grönberg from:
     Allan Bäckman CV
     SVENSKA DAGBLADET 30 Aug 1956
     SVENSKA DAGBLADET 1 Sep 1956 (x 2)

07. This   paper   was   published   in   17DE   SKAND.
     NATURFORSKAREMOTET 1923, pages 142 to 153. At the back

of the paper, there were tables of the daily readings which have been compared these with what was recorded in 1972/73.

	Average Temperature Bäckman's Method C	Average Temperature Seewarte's Method C	Average Minimum Temperature C	Total Rainfall mm
January 1921	9.2	9.8	6.0	618
January 1973	9.3	9.7	7.3	643
22 Dec '20 – 8 Feb '21	8.7	9.3	5.9	1023
22 Dec '72 – 8 Feb '73	9.7	10.0	7.5	812

In summary, whilst the month of January was similar for both expeditions, the periods 22-31 December and 1-8 February was significantly wetter for the Swedish expedition. During full period, the Swedish expedition experienced 26% more rain. The data below is for Cabo Raper. December 1920 and February 1921 were definitely wetter than January 1921. In December 1972, most of the rain fell before 20th December.

Cabo Raper	December	January	February
1920-21	231	153.6	185.3
1920-21 % above monthly mean	43%	-8%	30%
1972-73	448	298	167.3

The average temperature experienced by the Swedish team was lower at Camp 1, partly because of the lower minimum temperatures but also due to the wetter (and hence cloudier) conditions. Of interest is the lower minimum temperature. The Swedish camp was nearer to the glaciers than the British camp so the effect of cooling air from the glaciers at night was more significant.

08.   Allan Bäckman photograph when he was the Consul at Malmo

✧
Epilogue and the Changes

01. Reichert, F.. *La exploración de la Cordillera central patagónica desconocida entre los paralelos 46°30 hasta 47°30. Cerro San Valentín, informe preliminar de la expedición Hicken-Reichert* [artículos de revistas]. 1921. Publicado en: Sociedad Argentina de Estudios Geográficos. GAEA. Anales, I, 1 (2), pp. 3-23.

02. Refer to Note 07 of Chapter 2.

03. References include:

    Agnew, C.H. and Gobey C.S. *The Joint Services Expedition To Chilean Patagonia 1972.* The Geographical Journal , Jun., 1974, Vol. 140, No. 2 (Jun., 1974), pp. 262-268.

    Agnew, C.H. *The Joint Services Expedition To Chilean Patagonia 1972/1973.* The Joint Services Trust Committee 1974.

04. Shipton, E. *Crossing The North Patagonian Ice-Cap.* Alpine Journal, 1964, pages 183-190.

05. Agnew, C.H. *Map-making on the Patagonian ice-cap.* Geographical Magazine, Sept 1974, pages 710-713.

06. Subsequently Raleigh International. Refer https://en.wikipedia.org/wiki/Raleigh_International. Prince William participated in the Chilean branch in 2000. The Chilean phase was wound up in 2006.

07. Work published as a result of these expeditions include:

    Winchester V and Harrison S. *Recent oscillations of the San Quintin and San Rafael glaciers, Patagonian Chile.* 1996. *Geografiska Annaler* 78(A), (1): 35-49.

    Harrison S, Warren CR, Winchester V and Aniya M. *Onset of rapid calving and retreat of Glaciar San Quintin, Hielo Patagónico Norte, southern Chile.* 2001. *Polar Geography*, Vol. 25 (1), 54-61.

08. Refer to Note 05 of Chapter 5.

09. https://glaciar-benito.cl. Work published as a result of this expedition is:

Winchester, V. et al. *Post-1850 changes in Glacier Benito, North Patagonian Icefield, Chile*. 2014. *Geografiska Annaler* 96(A), (1): 43-59.

10. http://www.antofaya.com/explorers2

11. https://glaciar-benito.cl. Work published as a result of this expedition is:

Ryan, J. C. et al. *Rapid Surface Lowering of Benito Glacier, Northern Patagonian Icefield. Front. Earth Sci.,* 01 May 2018.

✧
Acknowledgements

F irst and foremost, I am indebted to Ulf, Unn and Åsa for the provision and translation of H N Pallin's articles, the subsequent checks and corrections, the use of photographs including additional ones in their own collections and subsequent support.

John Hendeström has been invaluable in enhancing this book, firstly by allowing the use of extracts from his grandfather's diary/letters to provide additional narrative for the expedition and then providing me with many additional photographs and support.

My thanks go to the following institutions and organisations:

- University of California, Special Collections at Santa Barbara for the provision of scanned sheets of H N Pallin's third album. An especial mention for Daisy for her invaluable help.
- UK Hydrographic Office at Taunton for the copy of the original 1830 chart and other relevant material.
- University of Gothenburg Library for access to Professor Otto Nordenskjöld's archives including many photographs and other materials. In particular, Anders Larsson has been most helpful.
- Mitchell Library of New South Wales in Sydney for the examination of Pringle Stokes last journal and the reproduction of material from that journal.

- Scott Polar Research Institute Library at Cambridge, England
- Royal Geographical Society Library in London.
- Gothenburg's Natural History Museum for information relating to Sten von Rosen.
- The *Alpine Journal* (the Alpine Club) for extracts from H N Pallin's 1933 article.
- Discovery Air Helicopters, Chile for the flight around 'Big Top'.
- Armada de Chile (Chilean Navy) for 100 years of support of expeditions to Kelly Inlet

The individuals who have helped me on this path are many so please excuse my omission if you have not been mentioned. The support that has been provided to me for the Patagonian expeditions together with much other advice by Olaf Wündrich and Jammie Valdivia has been immense. Professor Stephan Harrison provided me with the write-up of his trips to Glacier San Quintin as well as other hints. Crispin Agnew allowed me to use his article in the *Geographical Magazine*. Camilo Rada prompted me to start the journey of discovery and provided me with other invaluable leads. The project would not have happened without the diligence and expertise of Johan Grönberg. Flynn O'Shaughnessy made the first collection of material from Professor Otto Nordenskjöld's archives for me.

Then there are the many participants of the five expeditions and trips that I have taken part in to this amazing region, which has given me a small understanding of the physical environment, together with the organisations and individuals that have supported those endeavours:

- British Joint Services Expedition to Chilean Patagonia 1972/73.

- Feasibility investigation for expedition to Glacier Benito in 2006.
- Glacier Benito Revisited expedition in 2007.
- Glacier Benito Revisited expedition in 2011.
- Glacier Benito Revisited expedition in 2017.

Research could not have been undertaken easily without Internet-based sources. The first is Wikipedia. The next are the search engines. The third set of sources relates to 'free' online books and articles that have been scanned including the 'Wager' books, Steffen's books and the Narrative of the Surveying Voyages . . . The fourth set of sources relates to specific information made available on the Internet such as the Cabo Raper Lighthouse railway, the Istmo de Ofqui Canal Cutting, Google Earth, MapCarta etc.

Many individuals have helped me with the production of this book. Special acknowledgements go to Amber for the production of the maps and Andrea for a comprehensive read of the draft document.

✧
The Photographs

All undated black and white photographs are those taken by Professor Otto Nordenskjöld, Nils Pallin, Allan Bäckman and possibly Sten von Rosen and are acknowledged accordingly. It is not possible to attribute these photographs to an individual photographer as often several copies exist in the different archives.

Unless stated specifically in Notes, all 1972/73 photographs are attributed to members of the Joint Services Expedition to Chilean Patagonia 1972/73. All 2007 photographs are attributed to members of Glacier Benito Revisited 2007 expedition. All 2011 photographs are attributed to members of Glacier Benito Revisited 2011 expedition and all 2017 photographs are attributed to members of Glacier Benito Revisited 2017 expedition.

About the Cover

Background photograph – part of the Patagonian Cordillera taken from above Co. Caldenius in April 2017. On the left is Mt. San Valentin. On the right is part of Glacier Benito whose surface has lowered by 130 metres since the photograph below was taken.

A similar view of the background photograph taken from the summit of Co. Caldenius on 5th February 1973. A permanent snow patch was present in the foreground.

Inset photographs (left to right, top to bottom).
1. Nils Pallin and Allan Bäckman whose stories are in this book.
2. Members of the 1921/22 Swedish Expedition to South America.
3. Glaciers Andrée and Frænkel flowing from the Cordillera in 1922.
4. The valley where Glacier Rabot used to be in 2017.
5. Glacier Rabot in 1922.
6. The 'empty' valley where Glaciers Andrée and Frænkel used to be in 2017.
7. The 2017 expedition members in front of their transport.

✧ About the Author

Martin Sessions, as a 24 year old Royal Navy Engineer Officer, spent five months monitoring a west flowing glacier of Chile's North Patagonian Icefield, one of the many tasks undertaken by the five month 1972/73 British Chilean Patagonian expedition. Returning on a reconnaissance in 2006, he was instantly struck by the dramatic changes occurring to the region's glaciers.

In 2007, 2011 and 2017, he led expeditions to observe the significant changes and measure the rapid surface lowering of the 1972/73 study glacier.

Aware that the 100 year anniversary of Professor Otto Nordenskjöld's Swedish South America expedition was approaching, Martin searched worldwide for stories, information and photographs to document how the region changed before and since the 1920/21 Swedish expedition.

www.ingramcontent.com/pod-product-compliance
Lightning Source LLC
Chambersburg PA
CBHW062120020426

42335CB00013B/1035